Three Loves

Graceann K. Deters

GRAND
SIERRA
PUBLISHING

Incline Village, NV

Copyright © 2016 Graceann K. Deters

Published by Grand Sierra Publishing
774 Mays Blvd. #10-452
Incline Village, NV 89451

Cover and Interior Book Design by Monkey C Media
MonkeyCMedia.com

Publishing Consulting by Jeniffer Thompson, www.JenifferThompson.com
Editors: Jeannine Ouellette and Sophie Ouellette-Howitz

Printed in the United States of America

ISBN: 978-0-692-49934-4

Publisher's Cataloging in Publication Data

Names: Deters, Graceann K., author.
Title: Three loves / Graceann K. Deters.
Description: Incline Village, NV : Grand Sierra Publishing, [2016]
Identifiers: ISBN: 978-0-692-49934-4 | LCCN: 2016901512
Subjects: LCSH: Gay men--Fiction. | Gay men--Family relationships--Fiction. | HIV-positive gay men--Fiction. | Closeted gays--Fiction. | Gay immigrants--United States--Fiction. | Families--Fiction. | BISAC: FICTION/Romance/LGBT/General | FICTION/Romance/LGBT/Gay
Classification: LCC: PS3604.E767 T57 2016 | DDC: 813/.6--dc23

To my three wonderful daughters, Angela Deters, Elizabeth Rohde, and Martha Harris, who helped me accept personal differences, while constantly questioning the "whys" of my good intentions.

TABLE OF CONTENTS

ACKNOWLEDGMENTS

At one point while writing this story, I was ready to stop. I shared my feeling with my ghostwriter, Jeannine Ouellette, and she asked me to think about why I started writing this story in the first place.

After giving this a great deal of thought, I came to the following conclusions: Having come from a very fundamentalist background, where every single word of the Bible was believed to be inspired and mandated by God, I had to deal with my beliefs about homosexuality. Ironically a dear friend recently said, "I'm changing church affiliation because our present church is drifting away from the teachings of Jesus, you know, like saying it isn't a terrible sin to be homosexual."

Meanwhile, I have met and have many friends who are gay. Also, some close friends of my three daughters are openly gay. And the sad truth is that I know many homosexual individuals who have, at some time in their lives, considered suicide. Studies show a high rate of attempted and completed suicide among homosexuals. Not only do many gay people go through periods of depression and confusion, but often their families struggle to accept sexual differences, especially if this contradicts their core religious beliefs.

This is why I wrote this book. That is, to offer a different opinion on the biblical views of homosexuality. In no way do I imply that I have all the answers. It is not my aim to say that those who disagree with me are wrong. This book is an attempt to show loving and meaningful relationships both among same-sex men, and loving and caring women.

This book is fictional. It is a novel. The story is from my imagination, though it is inspired by my life experience. My inspiration for the various characters in this book came from people I have known throughout my life. Yet the opinions, interpretation, and storytelling are all mine. I take full responsibility for this novel and hope that this book will be of help and inspiration to others.

I have many special people who helped me along the way. The first person I contacted was my daughter Martha's close friend, Santiago Lopez. Martha met Santiago while they were attending the University of Michigan. Both were active in the drama department. I knew Santiago was openly gay and a devout Roman Catholic. He also informed me that he had been a Jesuit aspirant, discerning his calling to the Jesuits. Santiago answered my many questions, especially about Padre Antonio. For example, I wanted to know how Father Antonio would pray, and whether his character seemed real. Santiago said, "Wow, that was pretty intense. Your character Maria is so tragic and I can see where her priest would be so torn about breaking the confidence of the confessional." Santiago was a caring, loving man, and it was a sorrowful moment when I received notice that he had died at the young age of forty-five on February 24, 2015. I feel honored to have known this great person.

Rick Hughes, who has published four books, gave me an honest critique of my story and was able to correct some of my errors and at the same time give me encouragement to continue writing.

Charles Grande is a priest of the American Catholic Church and was a great help. He has written an autobiography about his own experience as a gay man in seminary in the 1960s, and his book has been made into a movie. He especially helped me interpret how Padre Antonio would speak and think. His correction and additions were invaluable.

The priest in our Episcopal Church, Eric Heidecker, is openly gay. He gave a new and different perspective in his critique of my story and helped me to better interpret the gay lifestyle and a priest's interpretation of God's word.

Some of the most helpful and honest feedback came from Linda Brown. I asked Linda to critique the story from a heterosexual and female point of view, which she was able to do in marvelously creative ways. I have great admiration for Linda as a teacher and also for her Christian point of view on homosexuality. She helped me to better understand my purpose for telling this story. She gave suggestions on how to develop more depth in the relationships between the characters.

I could go on and on with many details about the wonderful help I received from many people. William Pereira, a pilot, helped figure out details of the flight from Miami to Brasilia. Kathy Harmon was right on track when she gave constructive criticism of Betty, noting that Betty's unflappable good nature was unbelievable. "If the Pope knew her," said Kathy, "she would be canonized for being so saintly!" So I went back to the drawing board and overhauled this character.

I want to thank my family including my three daughters, Angie Deters, Beth Rohde, and Martha Harris, not only for their help in developing my characters, but also for listening to me and for their understanding and acceptance of their wonderful gay friends. I also thank my husband Bill, who corrected my grammar and gave constructive help when I asked, and sometimes when I didn't ask. I knew I could trust his judgment and he added a great deal to this story.

Last but not least, I could never have tackled this project without the help and support of my ghostwriter, Jeannine Ouellette, and her daughter Sophie Ouellette-Howitz. Not only did they add color to the manuscript, but they provided encouragement when I needed it the most. I'm grateful for everyone who has been a part of this process.

Atlantic Ocean

Equator

Amazon River

Manaus

Belem

Brazil

☆ Brasilia

Tropic of Capricorn

São Paulo

Rio de Janeiro

Itajaí
Florianópolis

Porto Alegre

Pacific
Ocean

South Atlantic Ocean

N

South America

0   100   200   300   400   500   600   700   800

Scale in Miles

River - - - - - - - - -

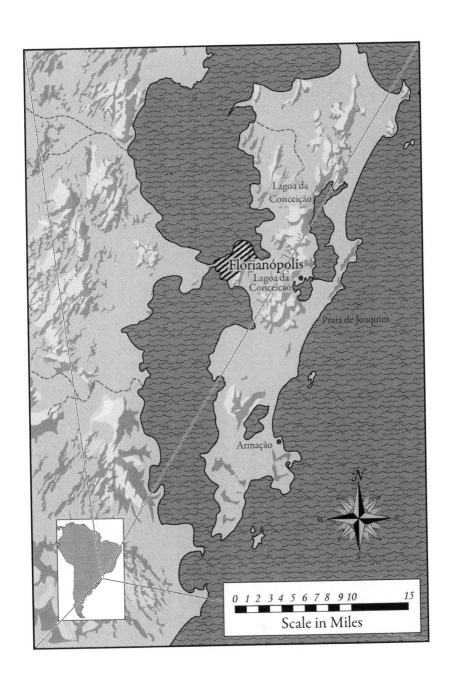

Lagoa da
Conceição

Florianópolis
Lagoa da
Conceicao

Praia de Joaquim

Armação

N
W   E
S

0 1 2 3 4 5 6 7 8 9 10   15
Scale in Miles

PROLOGUE

Everything looked familiar, and yet nothing was the same. As I drove through my old neighborhood, I saw new storefronts here and there but the blocks still matched the memories I had. What was different, what had changed, was me.

I slowed the Corvette as I neared my destination. Unsure of the store's exact location, I tried to spot Betty's stalwart Taurus. The irony of my situation hit me like the first rush of a strong drink: I was shopping for baby cribs with my wife. If someone had told me a year ago—hell, even a month ago—that I'd be returning to Miami as a father, I'd have laughed myself sick. Now here I was, back from Brazil with two babies in tow. Yes, two. A first-time father twice over. Twin miracles.

I followed Betty into the parking lot and circled the rows, searching for a space. There was one, but thanks to a minivan parked on a sloppy diagonal, it would be a squeeze. Anthony would kill me if I scratched the paint. And, I realized, we were going to have a hard enough time loading the cribs without having to maneuver them past neighboring cars. Suddenly I envied the minivan's spacious interior and sliding doors. Though I was anxious to finish the shopping excursion and return to Anthony and our babies, I drove on.

Once inside, Betty took charge. She enlisted a store manager, and we moved from display to display, the two of them trading informed opinions on cribs, changing tables, and something called a "Diaper Genie." The manager keyed in on my dazed expression. "Don't worry, Dad," he said. "Your wife knows what she's doing." Betty smiled like a cat with a bellyful of canary.

I pointed at the plastic canister with its puckered lid. "Not to be rude, but that's just tacky. I couldn't stand looking at it every day, and I know Anthony would agree."

Now the manager was the one with a dazed expression.

"Don't be difficult, Bruno," Betty said. "Parenting is about what's practical, not what's pretty."

"You know what they say," the manager chimed in, "happy wife, happy life." He forced a chuckle.

"Trust me, 'they' weren't thinking of me when 'they' came up with that saying."

I angled the cart toward the round racks of baby clothes and pushed it, hard.

Soon enough, Betty appeared by my side. She silently flipped through the tiny hangers, pausing occasionally to consider various pastel-colored playsuits.

"You were that set on the Diaper Genie?" I said, finally.

"They're your babies, living at your condo. It's your choice."

I sighed. "I want your input, Betty, but it is my choice."

"Because you're so qualified to be making decisions about the welfare of two infants? What you know about childcare could fit on the nail of my pinky finger."

"I know enough to know there are lots of things I don't know! That's the whole reason I asked you to come shopping with me! I want all the help you're willing to give."

"Too bad you didn't ask Rosa. I'm sure she has plenty of help for you."

"Oh, so that's what this is about?"

"I just don't see why you always have to involve her! I mean, our marriage may not be the most traditional, but I am your wife. Just because I don't have children of my own? You know I was the oldest of four. I raised my two brothers and a sister. I was practically a single mom, with all the dressing and shopping and feeding I did while my parents were on the road."

"I do know, but I forget sometimes. Can you blame me? You never talk about your childhood, or your family."

"It's in the past." She rested her hands on the curved metal bar of the rack. "The point is," she said, looking at her hands, "I know at least as much about kids as Rosa does."

"And that's why you're here with me now." I put my arm around her shoulders. "I'm glad we're doing this together. I'm so in love with the twins, and so terrified I'll do something to fuck this up. I want you by my side, Betty."

She turned her face to me and, with a slight smile, said, "And that's where I plan on being. Now focus. We have a lot to do."

∾

CHAPTER ONE

Where Do We Go From Here

I never saw it coming, even though I was deathly sick all through January of 1993. The cold, which had a bitterness that felt personal at times, had gotten into my bones. I spent five days in bed wracked with fever and nausea. Those days are scored into my memory, hieroglyphs I only learned to read looking back.

I was doubled over in pain, crawling back and forth from my bed to the cold, white tile bathroom. Anna, my wonderful "American mother," worried and watched over me, bringing ice and Tylenol and washcloths to keep my temperature down, and staying by my bed as I shook uncontrollably under a thick stack of blankets. By the fourth day, I improved slightly. By the fifth day, I managed to keep down small bites of bland food. Fortified by chicken broth and dry toast, and by Anna's firm hands on my elbow, I even climbed weakly out of bed.

Oh, Anna. Bless her heart. She was convinced the reason the flu hit me so hard was because I had lived my whole life in Brazil and had never been exposed to the virus before. "You just have no immunity against these terrible northern bugs," she insisted. I figured then, in the blissful haze of ignorance, that she was right. And by February, my health was perfect again.

It's unbelievable, now, to think of how quickly I dismissed the sickness. Of course young people have the right to believe in their own invincibility. But there was no safe way for a guy to have sex with another guy in Brazil in the 1990s, even for guys more committed to safeguarding their health than I had been. Being gay in Brazil was, in and of itself, a serious hazard. No condom could protect you if you were found out. Already, some men and women were fighting proudly to change that. Not me. I hid. Homosexuality, activism, HIV—all three terrified me. The others who felt how I did, we accepted dark corners and back rooms as our birthright.

In the United States, the atmosphere was lighter. Quite literally, the back rooms were better lit. Not to mention the La Femme showroom where I watched Dee Dee Richards dance—the first drag queen I ever saw in the flesh. Outside the bars, things were better too. Even the police force in Minnesota was, well, nice. Niceness had no effect on HIV, though, which was claiming lives just as greedily in the U.S. as in Brazil. One consolation was the booklet mailed by the Surgeon General to every single household telling citizens to fight the terrible disease of AIDS rather than attack its victims.

I held onto the thought of that booklet as I careened into Anna's and Jim's driveway to tell them my terrible news. It was 22 degrees above zero but it felt like 22 below. The wind coming across Lake Minnetonka rattled the windows of my VW bug as I cut the engine at the end of the long driveway. Dense clouds hid the sun so that the entire sky and the lake below it were the same color of dove gray.

The wind was cutting straight through me as I stood outside Anna's and Jim's wide oak doors. Through the graceful etched windows that framed the doors, I could see into the foyer and beyond it to the kitchen, where Anna stood at the stove over a sauté pan. When I finally pushed the door open, the smell of onions frying was strong and soothing. It reminded me of both Brazil and America, my two homes. On the counter next to the stove was some kind of meat—probably pork chops—awaiting the pan. To the left, in the sunroom, I could see the back of Jim's head. Finally, I willed myself to step in through the door just as Anna turned from her cooking and walked toward the foyer.

I slammed the door twice, using my full body weight to secure the latch against the force of the wind. When I looked up, Anna's face rearranged itself into a mosaic of fear.

"Bruno," she said. "What is it? Are you OK? Were you in an accident? The roads—."

"No accident." I wanted to give her a smile, a hug, anything that would feel normal and reassuring for both of us. But I just couldn't. "Anna? I need to talk to you and Jim together."

She gestured toward the sunroom. "Jim's right there, reading the paper," she said. She walked to me briskly, took me by the arm, and pulled me through the French doors. "Jim," she said, "Bruno needs to talk to us—together." She shivered suddenly. The cold air was seeping out of me and into their safe, warm house. Anna and Jim had shown me nothing but love and generosity, and in return, I was delivering nastiness into their home. Sweat broke out across my hairline, my chest, my lower back, even the hollows behind my knees. Anna arranged herself slowly and carefully beside Jim on the wicker loveseat.

"Bruno, my man," Jim said, his smile broad as always. He arranged his arm easily over Anna's shoulder, exuding cheer and comfort despite Anna's obvious distress and my own. "Sit down. Tell us what's on your mind."

"I'd rather stand," I said. I stayed on the other side of the glass coffee table, facing two of the people I loved most in the world. Anna's features contracted even more. "I'll say this as quickly as I can. You both know I've been working on getting my visa changed from visitor to temporary resident here in America. They've been so helpful at the St. Paul immigration office, especially Betty. Betty Monroe, I told you about her, we've become friends. Anyway, what I'm saying is, everything looked good, I was totally on track for my visa, until . . . well, until the blood test." I stopped and looked at my hands, noting the way the veins stood out, carrying my blood back to my heart. Had the grandfather clock in the foyer always been so loud? The room was shaking with its violent ticking.

Jim took off his reading glasses and set them on the newspaper, which rested gently on the pristine glass of the table.

"I don't know how to say this other than to just say it. The test results came back positive. For HIV."

The smell of onions was suddenly sharp, burning. Anna started to cry.

"Did you know? Did you suspect?" Jim asked.

"There was that bout of flu in January. But other than that? I've felt fine. I had no idea. The test, all of this, it's a total shock to me."

"Bruno," Jim said. He picked up his glasses. "Do you have any idea how this happened? How you got this virus?"

The onions were definitely burning. Did I have any idea? No, and yet, how could I not? I rolled back my shoulders and faced Jim and Anna like a man. "There's something you don't know about me," I said. "Something I've never said aloud, although if I'm being honest I've known it for years—."

Jim started to say something, but Anna raised her hand, and he stopped.

"I'm attracted to other guys," I said.

Again Jim opened his mouth, but before he could form a single word, Anna placed her hand firmly on his shoulder and he shut it again.

"It's more than just feelings. I won't go into details, and I, well, I don't know for certain, but there was a hair stylist—he, I, there was an affair right before I left Brazil. I haven't heard anything more from him or about him, but maybe . . . ."

"Bruno, we love you," Anna said. She was blinking fast. Her lips moved and nothing came out. "Nothing could ever change that," she said finally. "But we need to know what this means. For the visa. Will you have to return to Brazil?"

"I don't know—I'll go back to the immigration office on Monday. It's hard to think. And my parents can't know! They can't, OK? I need you to promise." Anna and Jim looked at each other.

"The onions," Anna said. She stood and walked toward the kitchen.

"Jim, please," I said. "I know my parents are your dear friends, I know this isn't an easy secret to keep, but you have to understand. For them, in Brazil, AIDS is like—like leprosy. My family will shun me! No one will want anything to do with me. This would destroy my parents. Keep this secret, for their sake."

Anna came back through the French doors. She leaned on the arm of the couch. Jim patted the seat beside him, but she shook her head. "I think you're right about your parents," she said. "For now, at least. But in time . . . well, we'll see." She looked at Jim. "The thing we need to do first is figure out what to do, how to help. We have to take action, Jim."

"I can write a letter to the immigration office," he said. "I have friends and business associates who could be influential." He took Anna's hand. I appreciated the offer, but the grim set of Jim's mouth confirmed what I already knew. No amount of influence could overcome the law preventing foreign nationals carrying the HIV virus from obtaining resident visas. Tears streamed down Anna's face and dropped onto her light blue skirt.

The smell of burnt onions hung acrid in the air.

∿

Chapter Two

Homelands

As the youngest of my siblings, I was the last to be sent to America to live with Jim and Anna. Anna was my father's dear friend and cousin, and Jim was her husband. By the time I arrived in Minnesota in June of 1992, I had spent over a decade anticipating my turn for what my family had come to call the "Great American Visit." I'd heard the stories of our families' connections time and time again.

Anna's grandfather, Hans Miller, had originally emigrated from Germany to Itajai, Brazil. But he stayed in Itajai only twelve years before coming to the United States in 1908. He brought his three sons with him, but his youngest child and only daughter, Elizabeth, stayed behind in Brazil. Eventually, Elizabeth married and had three children—the youngest was Rudolfo, my father.

In 1950, during the aftermath of the Second World War, Anna's father Wilhelm Miller brought his wife Edna and his only daughter back to Brazil to visit Itajai. He was anxious to see his "baby" sister

Elizabeth again. He had not laid eyes on her since 1908 when Hans
had taken his sons to America. Both Anna and my father loved
to recount the story of that first meeting. Anna was sixteen years
old and my father was just one year older, but a whole world more
sophisticated. Anna was in awe of Rudolfo's experienced airs, and
he was dazzled by her American status. The two cousins hit it off
instantly, forming a friendship that would last the length of their
lives, though they never lived on the same continent.

Here is the point in the story where, in their own frequent
retelling of family lore, both Anna and my father would usually dash
away to dig out their stacks of old letters: pages and pages of faded,
flowing script that had traveled between Itajai and Minneapolis
over the years. My father's love for all things American thrummed
from those soft, cracked papers. "Anna," he confided early in their
letter-writing career, "someday soon I want to visit North America.
And not only that, I also know that when the day comes that I am
a father, I want my children to live in America." My father was
obsessed with American music, movies, fashion, politics, everything.
"What do you think of Frank Sinatra?" he'd write one week. "Is he
as popular in the United States as he is in Brazil?" If Anna had
written back saying no, my father's esteem for Sinatra would have
plummeted. Meanwhile, he'd be full of more questions: "What is
the most popular song in America right now? How are the most
stylish American men wearing their hair? What are the top cars to
buy these days?"

In addition to the home in Itajai, my grandparents had a
summer home ninety miles south on the island of Santa Catarina,
off the eastern coast. Santa Catarina is a natural paradise edged by
forty-two of Brazil's most beautiful beaches. A heavenly enclave

of tropical beauty. My grandfather built a charming, whitewashed cottage on one of the prettiest and most pristine stretches of coast, Armacao Beach. Along this expanse of sand and water, there were only summer homes and cottages. Most of the population lived on the northern half of the island. Armacao Beach, on the southern edge, was only forty minutes over rough gravel roads from Florianopolis proper, the capital of the entire state of Santa Catarina, which included not only the island but also a section of mainland Brazil.

In Florianopolis, my father was a popular and highly sought-after young man, a bit of a local celebrity even. Partly this was because of his voice—he sang beautifully and was a frequent guest performer on the local radio program. Back then, pretty much all of the locals were loyal radio fans. But with his piercing good looks, my father made an even bigger splash when he sang live, which he did whenever he had the opportunity. He loved nothing better than to wow the crowd and woo the ladies.

My father was onstage when he first laid eyes on my mother. It was New Year's Eve and he was performing at a local yacht club, crooning to a full crowd of locals who were literally glittering in their holiday finery. Laughter and cigarette smoke poured from the club's open windows into the inky night. When my father tells the story, he always insists that the reflection of the twinkling lights on the water's surface was so bright that you could read the names written on the bows of the boats. It was in that magical glow, as he belted out his favorite ballad in his most seductive baritone, that he saw her. My lovely young mother, Neuza. She was deep in animated conversation with friends, the bracelet wrapped around her tiny wrist flashing as her hands circled and swooped through the smoky air as she spoke. "Her beauty stunned me," my father said, "the amber waves of hair framing her oval face, her hazel eyes. And so petite! Like a pixie." My father always took great pride in my mother's daintiness. At five feet tall and no more than a hundred pounds, she had the perfect figure. A fact, he said, that was not unnoticed by the men in the room who were "circling her like moths." Undeterred by the competition, my father swept my mother onto the dance floor every chance he had, and by the turn of the next year they were married.

From the beginning, my parents seemed to enjoy unsurpassable luck in all that they set out to do. My father slid easily into a prestigious position with the state government in Florianopolis. That same year, my brother Ricardo was born—their golden boy. By their third anniversary in 1959, my father had been captivated by the rumblings he heard from legislators and their aids about plans for a new Brazilian capital. The officials hoped to nudge population growth from the coastal areas to the country's interior. If they could successfully establish a new capital city in the center of the country, they'd be one step closer to that goal. Should their plan go forward, all of Brazil's federal offices and employees would have to relocate from Rio de Janeiro to Brasilia. My father was convinced the family's future lay in Brasilia, a bright new city for two bright young things and their bright new baby boy.

On the very same day that my parents arrived in Goais, the central state where construction of the capital was underway, job offers started pouring in at my father's feet. Ultimately, he would play a pivotal role in establishing Brasilia as the new seat of the nation's government. From its inception, the vision for the capital city was complex. Brasilia was designed to be a futuristic city—

the dream of President Juscelino Kubitschek. Kubitschek and his cabinet commissioned architect Oscar Niemeyer and urban planner Lucio Costa to construct a city in the shape of an airplane or, some say, a butterfly. Each wing functioned as a distinct sector of the new city: the hotel sector, banking sector, embassy sector, and so on. The fuselage held the government offices and all federal buildings. Apartments and various residences were built in numbered blocks in the fuselage as well as the sectors.

As manager of the relocation effort, my father oversaw the entire daunting task of transferring staff and structures from Rio de Janeiro to Brasilia. His office handled housing and moving arrangements for all government and congressional leaders and their staff. He executed his responsibilities with great aplomb, and by the time Brasilia was inaugurated on April 21 of 1960, everyone recognized the name Rudolfo Garcia as that of a man who was a respected and valued member of Brasilia society. My mother accepted a position as office manager to the general contracting company for the city. Like all middle- and upper-class Brazilian women at the time, my mother had a full staff of servants—maid, cook, nanny, gardener, and more. She could work, socialize, and volunteer as much as she wished, and she did.

My father took a risk, betting on the success of an unusual city that some were sure would never amount to anything. As it so often did for him, my father's daring paid off. Despite widespread skepticism—many predicted a swift collapse and governmental retreat to Rio de Janeiro—Brasilia became the fourth largest city in Brazil with a sprawling population of nearly four million. Built from the ground up in less than four years from start to finish, Brasilia thrived.

Those early years were a whirlwind of exhaustion for my parents. My father's letters to Anna grew scarce, but never stopped altogether. In the fall of 1960, he sent her news of another baby:

November 30, 1960

Dear Cousins Anna and Jim:

I hope you are well. Neuza is happy with the new baby Rosa Anna Brito Garcia, born July 6. What do you think of that middle name? She came just after the many celebrations for the inauguration of Brasilia concluded, after carrying on for two months, April and June. I'm very tired now.

But I tell you the wonderful time I had last week. I went to Rio de Janeiro for some work, and a friend—Senator Vitorino Freire—asked me to a party at his house Saturday. Anna, we did not talk of the new Brazilian music, but Bossa Nova is all over Brazil, I hear in America it is popular too.

You cannot imagine my big surprise at the party when the great Antonio Carlos Jobim arrived. For the first time in my life, I was completely speechless. Jobim and Vinicius de Morais wrote the movie Black Orpheus and it won the Academy Award in Hollywood last year for Best Foreign Film. Jobim is very popular all over the world now. I was a little sad because Vitorino said Joao Gilberto was also to come to the party, but he did not. That was maybe more than I could stand. Joao is a big star here in Brazil. He sings and plays the guitar on beautiful Bossa Nova songs. You should go out now and buy his two popular records, "Disafinado" and "Chega de Saudades."

I think of you at the party and you would have a good time, too. When I visit you this summer I will tell more. Goodbye now.

Hugs from Rudi and Neuza

In her reply, Anna told my father that Jim went to a music store the very next day and ordered the two Gilberto 33s that Rudolfo had so heartily recommended. When the records arrived a week later, he played them morning, noon, and night. He couldn't wait to order more. Jim's love affair with Brazil had begun even before setting foot on Brazilian soil, and our cross-cultural appreciation club gained another member.

Chapter Three

The Great American Visit

I was twelve when my sister Rosa first went to America. She wrote home often, and to my great delight, she usually included a little treat for me along with her letter. Sometimes she sent Twix bars or whatever else was the latest fad candy. Once, very memorably, she enclosed a set of Captain Kirk and Mr. Spock action figures. These gifts sparked a fiery curiosity in me about my American family. I pestered my parents incessantly, demanding detail after detail, story after story, about the legendary Anna and Jim.

One day, I could no longer contain my curiosity as I stood near the china cabinet with my mother, watching as she carefully checked the condition of each piece of her prized—and extensive—collection of Flora Danica china. This was her annual tradition, scrutinizing and recording each piece for any chips or hairline cracks, mainly to ensure that our maids would exercise nothing but the greatest care in their weekly dusting. Finally, I got up my nerve to fire off the question I'd long wanted to ask: "Why don't I have any American cousins, like Dad does?"

My mother's quick hands stilled, the china plate she held in one and the notebook in the other hovering over the shelf. "You do," she said brightly, "Anna is your cousin, too."

"You know what I mean," I replied. "A cousin my own age who could visit me here, like Anna visited Dad? I want a cousin like that! We could write letters and everything. We could be real pen pals! Why don't I have that kind of cousin?"

My mother sighed. "Because, *meu filho*, the world is unfair sometimes. Anna can't have babies of her own."

"Oh," I said. Then, after a moment, "How come?"

"No one can answer that."

"Then how does she know?"

"She tried."

"Oh," I repeated. I had a sketchy idea of what trying to have a baby might involve, and that, combined with the sadness that had risen in my mother's face, was enough to stop my questions.

"Luckily," my mother said, her hands moving over the stacks of china again, a squeaky happiness in her voice, "I had three babies. And such demanding ones! You're far too much to manage on my own. Why do you think I'm always sending one of you off to Anna?" She tousled my hair, then smoothed it back into place and—gently cupping the back of my skull with her soft hand—she gave my forehead a kiss.

Ricardo's and Rosa's long stays in America with Anna and Jim gave them the chance to learn perfect English, and to feel almost as at home in America as they did in Brazil. No length of stay, however, was enough to get them adjusted to the northern climate.

Although both my brother and my sister loved Minneapolis, neither could handle the vicious winter cold. Still, their visits hooked them on the good old U. S. of A., and they just chose to live in its more southerly parts.

Ricardo eventually moved to Miami, Florida, where the winters—as well as certain "business opportunities"—were much more to his liking. He liked the 24-hour social scene too, and the scene liked him right back. My brother was a traffic stopper, no exaggeration. And if his looks didn't do you in, his charm would. As my sister always said, anyone, man or woman, who spends more than ten minutes in Ricardo's presence inevitably falls in love with him. Rosa would be the one to know because she had a similar effect on people. And after a short stint in Italy—just time enough, apparently, to attract a marriage proposal from the man who became her husband, Luigi Ferrari—she too moved to Miami.

I was twenty-five by the time I arrived at Anna's and Jim's, older than either of my siblings had been. At long last I was there on American soil. In my first weeks in Minnesota, Anna and Jim often remarked on my failure to show even the slightest hint of homesickness or, in fact, sadness of any kind. "He's too busy talking nonstop," Jim joked.

"Who does he remind you of, Jim, that thing he does with his hands when he talks?" Anna asked. She turned to me. "Surely you've heard it before? Your gestures are just like your mother's."

I dropped my arms to my sides.

"Now you've done it, Anna," Jim said. "No red-blooded man wants to be compared to his mother."

"Oh, no, I meant—it's charming," Anna blushed.

My gestures weren't the only trait of mine that Anna and Jim picked up on that had previously been unnoticed, even by me. They routinely called me handsome, a word I'd always reserved for men like my brother and father, with their Hollywood good looks, and even more importantly, their towering height. I was a mere six inches taller than my mother.

"I'll bet the young ladies are helpless in your presence," Jim would say. "I'm sure you've got them all swooning, just like your brother and father do."

I was not quite sure how to respond.

Talented was another surprising word Anna liked to use to describe me. It started, I think, with my cooking. Initially I had to coax Anna to let me into her sparkling suburban kitchen with its modern appliances and well-stocked pantry, but once she did, she said the dishes I made were so delectable that she was tempted to chain me to the stove. According to Anna and Jim, I had also inherited my father's musical abilities. "And then some," Jim would say. "Rudi never played an instrument the way you play that piano."

When Anna learned, after complimenting my pants, that I sewed my own clothes, she deemed me the Renaissance man, reincarnated. "It's truly unbelievable," she would say, shaking her head. "Is there anything you can't do?"

Once they learned I loved to dance, Anna and Jim insisted on taking me to a country western restaurant at the world-famous Mall of America in Bloomington, a western suburb of Minneapolis. They wanted to introduce me to line dancing, something unheard of in Brazil. As they suspected, it fascinated me. I was mesmerized by the intricate figures and shapes the dancers formed as they moved across the floor. I watched closely, turning away only long enough to scan the menu and place my order. While we waited for our food to arrive, I made my way onto the floor and fell into the line, moving with the other dancers, letting the thrum of music and feet moving in unison fill me.

When I returned to the table, Anna was shaking her head again in that way she had. "You looked as if you had been doing that your whole life."

"Didn't miss a damn beat," Jim said.

The only problem, really, with staying at Anna's and Jim's was transportation. Since Anna and Jim lived in Minnetonka, a suburb ten miles west of Minneapolis, I needed a way to get myself around. It just wasn't practical for my hosts, who both worked, to haul me wherever I needed to go—especially since I needed to go everywhere. I had serious exploring to do. Even if Anna's and Jim's schedules had permitted unlimited chauffeuring, I intended to keep some of my exploring to myself. So one of the first things I did that September was to buy myself some wheels. For $200, I purchased a 1970 VW bug. God, I loved that car.

Jim laughed out loud when he saw it. "What are you going to do with this wreck?"

In all fairness, the bug was a rusted out mess when I got it.

"You'll see, Uncle Jim. You won't recognize this baby in a few weeks. I can't count the hours I've spent in my Uncle Luiz's garage, watching men fix cars. Not just watching, I mean. I helped with the repairs, too."

I spent hours pounding and molding, and removing each dent until the body was completely smooth. I rented a spray machine and painted the exterior a dark green before attaching the new chrome fenders I bought. Neighbors and friends actually lined up to ogle over the refurbished interior. Flawless! What before had been ragged upholstery with crumbling foam stuffing escaping from gaping holes, now looked fresh from the factory. "Who knew your sewing skills would translate so well to car repair?" Anna marveled.

I even found a used VW engine for 75 bucks. I tore it down to nuts and bolts, cleaning each part meticulously before reassembling it like a huge, complicated puzzle. Once it was gassed up, the engine purred like a contented cat. "It's a work of art," Jim said. "Both the engine and the body." In the driver's seat, I was purring right along with the engine.

The single, serious point of contention I faced with Jim and Anna that first year was the topic of college. "I'm twenty-five, way too old for college," I said. "And way too restless." But my American parents would not relent. Once a week, at least, they circled back to the argument, pressing on with their laundry list of reasons why I needed to further my studies.

On occasion I came close to caving in, just to please them, but the truth was I had no interest whatsoever in college. I was interested in a different kind of education. American popular culture, for instance. I couldn't get enough of it. With each week and month that went by, I fell more deeply in love with the unlimited possibilities of this new country.

Anna and Jim treated me almost like a son, as if our family ties were closer than first cousins once removed. The question wasn't whether I wanted to stay on in America indefinitely, but how to make that a feasible prospect. Clearly I'd have to find a way to earn my own keep. I volunteered for odd jobs, but I couldn't be employed legally because I had only a visitor's visa and no green card. My father sent money as needed (which was often) with only minimal grumbling, but I had no desire to depend on his support forever. So I trekked to the Immigration and Naturalization Office in St. Paul to apply for a green card.

CHAPTER FOUR

A Real Proposal

Before the blood test, before a blandly official sheet of paper informed me that I was harboring HIV, before that three-letter label turned me into one of the walking dead, when I still believed that the biggest challenge ahead of me was simply to navigate the maze of government paperwork, I struck up a friendship with an immigration social worker named Betty Monroe. The first thing I thought when I saw Betty was that she looked utterly dependable—in a word, sturdy. And every interaction we had thereafter confirmed my initial impression. Betty was efficient, attentive, and adept as she oversaw the inordinate number of bureaucratic necessities involved in the immigration process. Despite her efficiency, those things take time, and thanks to my persistent chatting throughout it all, we formed something of a friendship.

Like me, Betty was twenty-five. That, however, is where our similarities ended. In most every other way, Betty was wildly different from me. Most notably, she was incredibly quiet—shy, is what I assumed at the time. And that seeming shyness was part of why I chatted her up to begin with; I've always felt a certain kind of tenderness toward shy people. How could a person not love to meet new people? To talk and laugh and dance and ham it up? Shyness seemed to me to be a kind of social disease, preventing those who had it from enjoying so many of the most enjoyable parts of life.

As we got to know each other, I learned that both of Betty's parents were over-the-road truckers. As the oldest of her siblings ("It's so obvious to me that you are the youngest," she said repeatedly), Betty had served as the default caregiver to her three younger siblings while growing up in southern Wisconsin, near the Illinois border. She had spent her years there counting down the days till she could finally leave home. This she told me with a sort of hardened grimness. It seemed fitting that Betty had the broadest shoulders I ever saw on a woman. As I said, sturdy. Homely, if I'm to be honest. This woman carried a heavy load. But through sheer grit, Betty managed to achieve an academic record impressive enough that the University of Minnesota offered her a full scholarship. She claimed to love the independence of being in the world, of finding her place. But to me, her life sounded downright lonely.

Eventually, it became clear that Betty had few friends. She got along with her co-workers, and was on decent terms with her neighbors, but she didn't have anyone she confided in or spent time with just for fun. One day, as we finished up some paperwork just before the office closed, I invited her out for a cocktail. "I'm sure you could use a drink after that ordeal," I said, "and I know I could." Soon enough, walking down the street for a drink became a habit. I found myself timing my visits to coincide with the end of her office hours. The fact was, I kind of enjoyed her company. Once I got a few drinks in her, Betty tended to lighten up. In fact, she could sometimes even be funny. Her humor had an edge to it, though—a very sharp edge. Betty's jibes about the workers and visitors in the Immigration and Naturalization Office could get me laughing until I cried. But more often than not, she saved her cattiest comments for herself.

She parodied herself so pitilessly that I could hardly catch my breath long enough to protest. "Betty! No!" I would guffaw. "I don't agree that you look exactly like Nicholas Cage wearing a blonde wig. I'm laughing at the absurdity of that idea, not because I agree!" As our friendship moved along, Betty opened up to me bit by painful bit. Humor, she once confided, was how she coped with her awkwardness and, as she put it, her ugliness. "I prefer to joke about myself," she said. "If I throw the first punch in my own direction, no one else will need to."

Despite my best efforts, Betty refused to accept any compliments about her appearance. One afternoon as I leaned against the counter, waiting while she filed away the last forms for the day, I noticed Betty was wearing a dress I hadn't seen before. Jersey knit, bias cut, with a tie in just the right place to define her waist. "That dress does wonders for your silhouette," I said.

"Please," she said, rolling her eyes. "Don't humor me, Bruno. I'm the ugly duckling who didn't grow up to be a swan—and we both know it. There's no lipstick or Wonderbra magical enough to turn me into a princess."

"It's not about magic, it's about choosing the right cut for your figure—."

"Not for me, it isn't. And that's OK, because even if it were, I'd still be too inept to talk to the kind of people who interest me. I've always been fascinated by the beautiful people. People like . . . well, like you."

I didn't know what to say.

When my blood test came back positive, Betty was more taken aback than anyone. But search as I might—and I certainly did—I found no disgust in her eyes. We were at our usual spot when I told her, a hotel bar just around the corner from the Immigration and Naturalization Office. I was terrified that my diagnosis doomed me to a return to Brazil. Perhaps I could tell my parents I had some other disease. Anything would be better than HIV. I still hated to even think of the word. I sucked the last drops of scotch off one of my ice cubes as I tried to catch the bartender's eye to order another round. I glanced at Betty's glass, and found it was still well over half full.

"Betty, don't you like the wine?"

She shrugged.

"I know you usually drink Chardonnay, but I thought Pinot Grigio might be even more your style."

"It's not that," she said. "This wine is great. I don't know anything about wine, I just order Chardonnay because I know how to pronounce it. But I like this one, this Pinot. Anyway."

She grabbed her glass with two hands and swallowed the rest of the wine in big, greedy gulps. Choking a little, she wiped away a dribble of wine with the back of her hand.

I laughed out loud. Her action was so out of character, I couldn't help it.

"Don't laugh. Or do. I just, I . . . Bruno." She blushed, as she so often did, but this time the dramatic patches of color that lit like small fires in her cheeks spread up her temples and into her hairline. "I have a proposal for you." She laughed nervously, at first, and then fully, loudly. It took her a minute to collect herself. "I have a proposal, Bruno. A real proposal."

"You would like to sell me a bridge in Brooklyn?"

"I would like to marry you."

I almost fell off the stool; I literally had to grab the edge of the bar to steady myself.

"Betty, I don't know how to, I thought you knew—."

"Oh, no, I do know," she said. "I know full well that you're gay."

"So you're joking?"

"Not in the slightest, I'm dead serious, in fact. Bruno, if you marry me, you'll get your green card and you'll be able to stay in America."

"But why? Why would you do this?"

"Look," Betty said. The color was still high in her cheeks. "I like you. You make me feel comfortable and not many people do. And if I don't marry you, I won't marry anyone." I started to protest but she stopped me. "Don't interrupt me, Bruno, and don't pity me. I need to say this all at once or I won't say it at all. But here's the truth. I have no illusions. I hate dating. I hate small talk. I hate parties, clubs, social gatherings of all kinds. It's so hard for me, Bruno. People aren't drawn to me. I've tried, but the fact is I'm just happier in a room with a book or the TV, and I'd prefer to be happy than miserable. But I don't want to be alone, either. Not forever, anyway. With no one to care whether I live or die? Why should it have to be that way when we both have something to gain from one another's company? I see no point in waiting around for 'true love,' if such a thing even exists, which I doubt. I know I'm no Cindy Crawford, and I think we can agree that the odds a stranger will sweep in and overlook my awkwardness are near to zilch."

"OK, maybe you're not Cindy Crawford," I said, "but who is? Except Cindy? You're you, Betty. You're Betty. And you're being way too hard on yourself. I noticed and remembered you the very first time I saw you."

"Just my luck," she said. "The only man who's ever noticed me turns out to be gay. I mean, that's the point, right? That's the whole thing, Bruno. I don't want to spend my life waiting. I want to do this for you, and I want you to think seriously about it. It's a sincere proposal. You could come and live with me." She paused. "I have a two-bedroom apartment, in case you're wondering. I understand exactly what our marriage— if we are to have one—will and won't be." Betty reflexively tipped her glass to her lips before remembering she had already drained it. She set her empty glass on the bar, tugged at the cuff of her blouse, then clasped her hands in her lap. "We get along so well," she said finally, as if that settled the matter.

As I walked out of the bar and down the hilly street to where I'd parked my car, I felt strangely detached from the ground. I felt like I was walking along the bottom of a swimming pool, weightless yet slow, like in a dream. The world around me blurred and wavered far more intensely than could be explained by three tumblers of scotch. It all seemed surreal, otherworldly. Betty wanted to marry me, even knowing that I was gay. Knowing that it would never be a real marriage. This was a loophole I'd never imagined. And yet, don't they always say that if something seems too good, it probably is? That troubling thought clouded my elation for a moment as I got behind the wheel before the tempting idea of a future in America, a future that might be possible after all, swept it away.

∼৴৲

CHAPTER FIVE

Something Blue

Nothing comes as quite such a joyous release as spring in Minnesota. Winter there is longer and harsher than even the locals can anticipate or remember until it happens again. By the time March thaws into April and April rushes toward May, elation reaches a fever pitch. People who have been trapped inside a dark and frozen snow globe for months on end respond as if spring truly is a miracle, an unprecedented spectacle of nature unfolding before their eyes. By the middle of May, when green leaves finally appear on the trees and sunshine at last warms the skin on bare arms, spring can feel exactly, beautifully perfect.

That was just the sort of spring day that greeted Betty and me on our wedding day. It was May 16, 1993, a sunny 73 degrees with just a gentle southwesterly breeze as we, the unlikely couple, walked hand in hand through downtown Minneapolis toward the courthouse. Betty wore a red sleeveless gown with a square neckline that perfectly accented her square shoulders. "Bruno!" she snapped when I first suggested I'd take her shopping for a dress. "Don't be an idiot. You're not supposed to see my dress before the ceremony."

"Betty, I know that sexual fidelity will not be a priority in our marriage. Remember, I'm a gay groom. And still you're marrying me. Do you really think those old myths apply to us?" She relented, and I took her to downtown Minneapolis to browse the big department stores. Inspired by Valentino's spring line, I suggested Betty choose his signature shade of red. She had been nervous about walking in a floor-length dress, but now, as her skirt shifted luxuriously with every step and the sun highlighted the sheen of the fabric, I could tell that despite her lack of good genes, she felt the way a woman should on her wedding day: beautiful. I wore a cream-colored suit, tailored to fit me to a T, with a red pocket square edged in black and a black bowtie. The ceremony itself was simple and swift, with just us two, the justice of the peace, and our respective witnesses. Betty asked her best friend, Marie, who stood beside her, dressed in a plain black shift, and I asked Manuel, a fellow Brazilian who knew of my diagnosis and understood better than anyone else the motivation behind our marriage.

I had managed to talk Anna and Jim out of coming to the courthouse—"You don't want to drive all the way downtown, fight traffic, pay for parking, just for five minutes in a dusty office of a courthouse!"—knowing that as accepting as they were trying to be of my situation, my marriage to Betty and its circumstances challenged their most dearly held beliefs about matrimony. I appreciated their steadfastness more than I could say, but couldn't stomach the thought of watching them try to smile during the ceremony.

Nonetheless, Anna had insisted on planning a wedding lunch

to take place afterward. As we exited the courthouse, I could feel Betty tensing up. I had only brought her to Anna's and Jim's once before. The whole experience had been wildly uncomfortable. If I had to guess, I'd say that their large, gracious house intimidated her. Her response was to bristle. "White carpeting and crystal, cloth napkins, two forks and two spoons, well isn't that just la di da," she said, once we were alone in the car. I may have shot back something about a small-town chip on her shoulder. It was our first real fight.

The luncheon was just the four of us seated around Anna's and Jim's expansive dining table, set with a perfect array of mouthwatering dishes that Anna had prepared herself and had arranged to serve in four leisurely courses. Betty was observably miserable through each and every course. Beneath her arms, which she kept pinned close to her body, her dress slowly darkened with perspiration. This was another of Betty's unfortunate genetic curses: she tended to sweat heavily in all of the worst circumstances. It was a pity. She tried only the tiniest nibbles of the delectable canapés, the mouthwatering salad Niçoise, the crisp-skinned and delectably seasoned broiled chicken, and the light-as-air lemon meringue pie.

Anna tried earnestly to engage her in conversation, but Betty's monosyllabic answers and prolonged pauses choked off every exchange. Neither could my interjections or verbal embroidery dispel the tension. I made social lubrication my top priority. By my fourth glass of wine, Anna was looking at me sidelong, but I pretended not to notice.

Didn't my diagnosis entitle me to enjoy myself as much as I possibly could? As far as I was concerned, if I was going to live with the threat of AIDS hanging over my head, I had a right to live in the moment and for the moment, to do more or less exactly as I wished. Thanks to Betty, I'd be able to live where I wished, as well. This thought filled me with a sudden tenderness toward her, even as she struggled now to respond with more than a stilted word or two to Anna's kindly questions.

The worst moment of the luncheon, by far, was the gift opening. We had moved from the formal dining room to the sunroom, which I hoped would set Betty more at ease. The afternoon light poured through the windows and bounced off the glass top of the coffee table. There sat a large, silver-wrapped box tied with a white satin bow. Anna was beaming. "This is for you, Betty," she said. "I so hope you like it."

Betty looked at the box as if it were a rabid animal, poised to attack her. Gingerly, she began to open it, barely touching the taped seams and being inordinately careful not to tear the paper, which she folded and set beside the carefully rolled white ribbon as if both might be needed on a future occasion. When Betty saw the box cover—inscribed with the Dayton's store insignia—she sucked in her breath. That elegant, downtown department store contained the purest, most untouchable luxury. She had never shopped there, not once. She lifted the lid of the box, and inside was a beautiful cut crystal bowl. Even with the lid not quite off, nestled within folds of snow-white tissue paper, the bowl's fine facets caught the afternoon light and bounced colorful prisms against the sunroom walls. "Well, well," Betty said, replacing the lid without even touching the bowl. Her lips drew together so tightly, they all but disappeared. It was as if now that she knew what the box contained, she was even less inclined to touch it than before. I gently took it from her and set it back on the coffee table.

"I'm—I mean, we're—overcome by your generosity," I finally said, as Betty sat in silence, unable to look at Anna. "I can't thank you enough."

One week later, I moved out of Anna's and Jim's house and into Betty's third-story corner apartment in a brick building near downtown St. Paul. I couldn't help but feel excited at the idea of moving into the city. Neither Anna nor Jim had tried to direct my comings and goings, but I was still looking forward to the independence of my new living arrangement. I loaded my few possessions, stuffed into cardboard boxes and brown paper bags, into the backseat of the green bug, humming nonsense tunes to myself as I did. Anna and Jim would have been blue about my departure no matter what, but their worries about my diagnosis made it even more difficult and awkward. I did my best to tamp down my own giddiness at moving out—it seemed disrespectful in the face of their sadness—and I tried to lift the melancholy by promising to visit as often as I could.

My parents arrived for their usual summer visit less than a month after I moved from Anna's and Jim's to Betty's apartment. This visit would, of course, be more exciting than usual because of my newlywed status. Anna arranged a dinner on Saturday evening, eager to facilitate my parents' introduction to Betty. But when I sped up the driveway in my refurbished bug, laying on the horn as I parked to announce my arrival, the passenger seat beside me was empty. My mother's tears started flowing the moment I wrapped my arms around her tiny waist. My father, too, gave me a big abraco— a gigantic Brazilian hug complete with kisses. "What about Betty?" Anna asked when the hugs and the tears subsided.

"She's not feeling well," I said. "She's heartbroken not to be here, but she didn't want to spread her germs around. And she really wanted to be at her best when meeting the two of you." I patted my mother's shoulder tenderly, hoping Betty's absence wouldn't dampen her happiness. Betty wasn't sick. Neither was she heartbroken to miss this very important occasion. The truth was, she had flat-out refused to come. And I wasn't in any hurry to force her to do anything she didn't want to do. After all, watching her at our wedding luncheon had been like watching a train wreck, and I wasn't eager for a repeat. Neither of us, we were realizing, had considered what it would be like to socialize as a married couple. For now, the best solution seemed to be for me to act as an ambassador on behalf of both of us, and for Betty to pout alone—or, for all I knew, down a few Chardonnays in front of the TV.

I was relieved to see that my parents absorbed the news cheerfully enough; it seemed that their genuine delight about my meeting someone and being married left little room for any disappointment. "This occasion calls for a toast," Anna said, as dinner drew to a close. "Jim, we need a bottle of bubbly!" My two sets of parents took turns toasting me, the lucky groom, and they even made several toasts to my absent bride. I promised to bring back the sentiments of those toasts to Betty and to repeat each one to her word for word, but I didn't really plan to keep that promise. The way I saw it, if Betty wanted to hear the toasts, she could have slapped on a smile and come along to meet my parents.

"And now I want the scoop on Ricardo and Rosa," I said to my mother. She more than anyone shared my love of gossip and drama, especially when it came to the doings and antics of my siblings. This time, however, she didn't take the bait.

"I'm afraid I'm fading fast, *meu filho*," she said. She stood up with her empty Champagne flute. "Rudolfo, I need to rest for a bit, and perhaps catch up on my letter writing. You will have to make the reports on Rosa's and Ricardo's doings for both of us."

My father rose to his feet and kissed her cheek. I followed suit. "You rest, mama," I said. "All that traveling, and lots of excitement! We'll catch up later." We walked my mother to the foyer stairs, and after my father gently took the delicate flute from her hand and set it back on the table, we adjourned to the sunroom. I held up the bottle, offering refills. Anna and Jim passed, but my father nodded and extended his glass. I topped off both of ours before settling into the loveseat. "Tell me about Rosa first," I said. "I need every last detail."

"Yes, tell everything!" Anna demanded, clapping her hands in exaggerated excitement. "I haven't had a letter from Rosa for more than two months."

Once the questions and conversation began to slow down, my father switched the subject midstream. "I can't stop thinking about the movie I saw last night in Miami," he said. "Maybe you've seen it—Philadelphia?"

"The gay lawyer movie?" Jim asked.

"He gets fired for being HIV positive," my father said. "Did you see it?"

"We're sure going to before it leaves the theaters," Jim said. "Anna's been talking about it for weeks—I hear Hanks is a shoo-in as a best actor nominee."

"I don't doubt it. The cast was outstanding, too—Denzel Washington and Roberta Maxwell. And the story, that's what I can't get out of my head. Hanks' character gets fired but he fights back, and he finds a lawyer willing to go to bat for him. Willing to risk his own career and reputation by defending a gay man."

"Thought-provoking story, to say the least," Anna said. With that she rose swiftly and rested her hands on Jim's shoulders. "So sorry, Rudolfo, but will you excuse us for a moment? Jim, I need you to do something for me. It won't take long." She shot me a look. Now is the time, she said with her eyes, just before she turned and left the room.

"Dad," I said, "what was your feeling about the Tom Hanks character? His being gay and having HIV?"

My father cleared his throat and lit a cigarette. "At least they still let me smoke in the sunroom," he said through his exhale, then tipped his head against the sofa and closed his eyes.

I waited.

"I guess I'm still sorting it out," he said finally. "Part of me felt repulsed by it all. Sick to my stomach. To think of two men together in that way, it's beyond unnatural. An abomination in the eyes of God, in the eyes of The Church and those protestants are even more upset about it than our priests." He paused to sip his Champagne. "But at the same time, I couldn't help but sympathize with the fellow for how he was treated. I think that's why I can't stop thinking about it."

My father sat up and propped his cigarette in the ashtray. The lines on his face were deep and many, and still he radiated health and vitality.

"Dad," I said.

He picked up his cigarette, dragged on it, and looked at me briefly before turning away. It dawned on me for the first time that my father already knew what I was about to tell him.

"I have something to tell you. Maybe it's not going to be a surprise. Either way it would mean a lot to me if you could still accept me after what I am about to say," I said. "Because I've lived with this for a long time and have wanted nothing more than for you to know this and still think of me as your son. Your son who is gay, but is still your son. Your son, the same as before."

My father took two more long drags. The only sound other than his inhaling and exhaling was the grandfather clock in the foyer. His hand and the cigarette he held in it shook and his eyes filled with tears as he stared hard into the distance through the paned windows of the sunroom. The sun had just dipped beneath the horizon, and dramatic red and yellow light streaked the sky outside. The elms in the front lawn stood in black silhouette against this fiery backdrop. "Bruno," he said at last, "You are married to a woman."

"Right," I said. "But Betty knows I'm gay. She was the one who proposed to me—right after I found out that I'm HIV positive. Oh, I didn't say that yet, did I? I have HIV. I found out when I applied for my green card. Betty wanted me to be able to stay in the United States, and that will be possible now thanks to this marriage."

"I feel sick for you, for her," my father finally said. "Sick for myself, as your father. Bruno, how could you allow this to happen? Any of it? And how could you take advantage of a young woman like this? This is a travesty in the eyes of God and The Church."

"It hasn't been my Church in a long time, Dad—if it ever was. And you're wrong about Betty. I can see how you would think I'm taking advantage of her, but she wanted to do this. It was for her sake, too. She's one of the loneliest people I've ever known. She's been alone for most of her life and she doesn't want to stay that way forever. I'm a friend to Betty. A real friend. You'll see that when you meet her. You can ask her yourself!"

"That's a good story you tell, Bruno, but if it's true, where is she now? Why would she not be here, sick or not? I find that excuse unlikely."

"You're right, I lied." I looked hard at my father's face, his dark eyes flaring with anger and hurt. The windows had turned reflective as the light left the sky, and I could see my own face over my father's left shoulder, my mouth set in a line, the mirror image of his. "I lied to protect Betty," I said, the pitch of my voice rising. I wanted to convince my father, but of what I wasn't completely sure. "Our unusual arrangement makes Betty feel especially uncomfortable around Jim and Anna. She'll be even more afraid to meet you and Mama when I tell her you know the whole truth."

"The HIV . . . ." My father stubbed out his cigarette and looked directly into my eyes for the first time since Anna and Jim left the sunroom. "I take it Anna and Jim already know?"

I nodded.

"I have nothing more to say right now," my father finally announced. His voice was drained of all the anger and edge it had held just a moment ago, a hornet without a stinger. "Except that your mother must not hear this under any circumstances. I may come to understand this, in time, but she never would. It would break her heart. It would destroy her."

"Why should you decide? I would prefer that my own mother know me for who I really am," I shot back. The force of my conviction surprised even me, because it was a conviction I didn't know I had. It had crystallized instantly in reaction to my father's demand for silence. "And I think she should know my diagnosis."

"There will be no negotiation about this, Bruno." Now his voice was inflating again, sharp and strangled in his throat. "I forbid you to devastate your mother with this. Forbid you! She is so happy and proud of your marriage—she's already talking about babies. The same goes for your so-called break from the Church. I don't want her to hear a word about it." He lit another cigarette and inhaled deeply. Just like that, he was transformed from hysterical to defeated. "Bruno, I too have news. I haven't told Jim and Anna yet, but your mother is failing. Fast. Last month the doctor told us . . . it's Alzheimer's. Early stages. But progressing quickly. So now you see why you must be compassionate for her sake. It's only decent to let your mother meet Betty and continue this fantasy you created."

We sat quietly in the darkened room, each weighing the measure of the other's news. When Anna and Jim slipped back in, I couldn't tell if a half hour or half the evening had passed. Anna turned on the table lamp and the room filled with yellow light. My eyes had adjusted to the dimness. It was harsh, almost blinding.

My father, with tears, repeated the news about my mother. "But please," he said as Anna wept into her hands, "let's change the subject. And Neuza must absolutely not find out about Bruno. I beg you to keep this from her. I implore you. I'm afraid this is her last trip to Minnesota, and I want it to be a happy one."

My parents met Betty the next day for lunch. "Oh, so sweet!" my mother exclaimed. "I'm blessed with another beautiful daughter. And I can have peace, knowing that Bruno finally has a wife." Betty squirmed in the circle of my mother's obvious delight, but at least this time she ate her food instead of picking at it, and she made an effort to participate in the conversation. If my mother noticed that Betty was less than beautiful or that her social graces weren't exactly glowing, she didn't let on. In fact, my mother was even more bubbly than usual, which made me love her even more. I found it difficult to reconcile my mother's energy with my father's dismal news.

But my mother's ebullience during those first days was deceiving. It became painfully clear by the end of the visit that my mother was very, very sick. She forgot dates and names of friends and muddled the details of past experiences. Then she would become agitated and angry. Saying goodbye was especially rough for Anna and Jim. They were uncertain if they would ever again see the Neuza they had known so well.

For this reason I felt even more guilty when, just days after my parents left, I shared more unwelcome news with my American parents. "Betty is requesting a transfer to Miami."

Anna's hands flew to her mouth. "Miami! And you will be leaving too?" Her expression made it obvious that she already knew the answer.

Another departure. Another goodbye.

"Betty's doing this mainly for me," I told Anna. "She says there's no way I will be able to weather another Minnesota winter, especially after hearing how sick I got last year."

Anna's face softened; the lines across her forehead smoothed and disappeared. She took my hands in hers and squeezed hard. "Of course," she said. "Of course. That is the most important thing—your health. And we can visit you in Miami and see Rosa and Ricardo at the same time. This is for the best."

Thanks to the glowing recommendation letter Betty's supervisor wrote for her, the transfer to Miami went through without a hitch. We made the move in the last week of July, just two months after our wedding. It was the height of Minnesota summer; the clean waters of Lake Minnetonka had finally grown warm enough for me to enjoy swimming. But instead, I loaded the bug for the long drive south.

Chapter Six

Miami Nice

When I called Rosa to tell her about the move, she insisted we stay with her until we found a place of our own. "Long distance realty?" she said. "Are you joking? You're asking for trouble. You'll stay with us." So we did.

The avalanche of hugs and kisses from Rosa and her husband Luigi and their two-year-old, Marlene (who only came up to my knee), set Betty at ease faster than anything I'd ever seen before. The cooing of the newest family member, baby Bridgette, didn't hurt either. Seeing Betty light up in the presence of nieces told me something about Betty that I had not known: apparently, she really liked children. This, I hoped, wouldn't present us with a problem as our "marriage" went on. After all, I use great care practicing safe sex, due to being HIV positive, and I for one didn't plan to be a father, ever! It occurred to me that perhaps these were the kinds of issues Betty and I should have discussed before we tied the knot. For now, though, it was just plain wonderful to see Betty smiling in the presence of my sister's little ones. Unfortunately, her all-too-familiar grimace reappeared as soon as I called my sister Mrs. Ferrari.

"Oh," Betty said. "Ferrari? Is Luigi from the car family?"

"Car family? What car family?" Rosa asked. She managed to keep a politely confused expression on her face for about thirty seconds before disintegrating into laughter. "Of course not," she said. "We'd be living somewhere grander than this little house if that were the case!" She swung her arm wide as if to embrace her homey but certainly not opulent surroundings. "Everyone thinks the same thing as soon as they hear Luigi's name. But in reality, his family owns a vineyard in Tuscany near Siena. It's nice enough, sure, but it's no luxury car factory."

On our second day in Miami, after she cleared away the breakfast dishes, Rosa unrolled a city map over the table. "The main thing you're going to have to think about is safety," she said. "That's number one. Anywhere you have drug trafficking, you have shootings and gang wars. And the rental neighborhoods are the worst of the worst. You have to be especially cautious in the rental neighborhoods."

Betty and I agreed that a one-year rental or lease was the best first step for us, though she'd always dreamed of owning her own home—and to my great surprise she'd already been saving toward a down payment for years. But being new to the city, she felt, and I agreed, it made more sense to rent until we had a better feel for Miami's neighborhoods.

"See here?" Rosa pointed to an area of the map labeled Little Havana. "This is one of the most dangerous neighborhoods in Miami. You couldn't pay me to live there. But then here," Rosa drew her finger slowly across the paper to a pink area labeled Kendall, "this neighborhood—nothing fancy, I'm not going to kid you, but it's safe and solid. You've got lots of families, good working families from Cuba, Puerto Rico, Brazil. All over South America, actually. It's relatively close to downtown and right on the Metrorail. This is somewhere you could feel at home."

It's funny that she put it that way, because I already felt more at home than I ever had in Minnesota. Even though I had slept on my sister's couch the last two nights, I felt oddly stable, at peace, but also exhilarated by the future. I loved the sensation of humid, oceanic air and the thrumming energy of the city.

I could see my sister was very happy here. She looked even more beautiful and luminous than ever, and that was saying a lot because my sister was a true knockout. I couldn't help but feel a little sorry for Betty when I looked at her next to Rosa, both bathed in morning light, one so glowing and the other so, well, haggard. More than once since we'd arrived, I'd observed Betty scrutinizing Rosa with a mix of envy and sadness. I couldn't blame Betty for envying Rosa, who was not only lovely, but also magnetic and charming. She and Luigi had moved from Italy to Miami just six months earlier, but already they'd established an extensive network of friends in their new community. "And it's going to be great to have you and Betty nearby, too," Rosa kept saying. These proud and somewhat overwhelmed parents—two-year-old Marlene and her baby sister, Bridgette, just three months old, kept them running at all hours—had longed to have family living nearby.

"Don't be greedy, Rosinha," I had teased her over breakfast the morning before, "you already have Ricardo here."

My sister's eyes lit up at the mention of our brother, then clouded over. "So to speak," she said. "It's a dream come true to be near him, but he's gone more than he's home. In fact, don't get too excited about seeing him, or introducing Betty. He left two weeks ago to bring his new yacht—you're not going to believe this one, it's like a mansion that somehow floats, way bigger and way shinier than his last one—down to Florianopolis to show Mom and Dad. And whatever else he's doing down there. Something about orange exports, he said. And of course his latest girlfriend, lucky girl, he's sparing no expense in showing her around Brazil. They'll apparently be sailing and diving in Fernando de Noronha, seeing Iguaçu Falls of course, and God only knows what else he's got up his charming sleeve. So I don't expect him back until January at the soonest."

"Any sign of a wedding ring on this one's finger?" I asked.

Little Marlene was eating cinnamon toast in tiny little bites while Bridgette slept peacefully in her baby swing. "I'll put my money on no," Luigi said, laughing. "You know your brother, Bruno. His heart of gold hasn't changed, but neither has his taste for adventure."

"And our life lacks adventure?" Rosa demanded, hands on her slim hips and mock anger in her eyes.

"Not in the least! What greater adventure could a man ever imagine than these two?" He planted a kiss on Marlene's cheek. "And you!" He swatted Rosa's ass. I was happy to see how in love they obviously were, despite the mayhem of parenthood. I turned to smile with Betty, only to see her lips tucked into a tight line. Whether it was Rosa's and Luigi's public display of affection, or the mention of Ricardo's yacht that had turned her stony, I wasn't sure.

Rosa, always empathetic, picked up on it too. "Don't let our show-off brother intimidate you, Betty," she said warmly. "He's a teddy bear at heart. You'll see." Rosa stopped suddenly and looked at Betty closely, up and down. "And when the time comes for you to meet him, we'll fix you up to make the best possible first impression." Betty looked shocked, almost as if she'd been slapped, but Rosa continued, oblivious, "My brother may be dripping in money, but life's not perfect for Ricardo. I was telling Luigi just the other day—well, we don't need to get into all that. The point is, Ricardo will love you just as much as we do. And you'll love him. You're one of us now, end of story. Right, girls?"

Marlene nodded with gusto, accidentally flinging a piece of cinnamon toast across the kitchen as she did. Bridgette slept on undisturbed in her swing, her little head lolled blissfully to the side.

Though Betty's affection for Marlene and Bridgette was clear, she remained strangely formal toward Rosa and Luigi. In the midst of my noisy, open-armed family, her reserve looked, well, outright rude. First she was cold with Anna and Jim, and now with my sister Rosa and her husband? My patience was wearing thin. And on top of that, there was the question of whether Rosa had or hadn't told Luigi I was gay. At least she knew the truth. When I'd phoned to tell her about the move, she had been curious to know why, and explaining our relocation without revealing my HIV-positive status would have required more tall tales than I was willing to tell.

It took me several days to finally ask Rosa outright about what Luigi did or did not know, but when I finally asked the question directly, Rosa handled it just as smoothly as she had when I initially told her. "Of course he knows," she said, "and he's totally fine with it. If he wasn't fine, I would have fixed that soon enough. But it was never a problem, not for either of us."

Soon Rosa demonstrated unequivocally that not only was she a loyal sister and a valuable social asset, but she was also an unrivaled house-hunting guide. She had spent many hours searching for the house that she and Luigi were now renting, and now had a detailed knowledge of the Miami housing market. We intended to start location scouting soon, and were poring over the map to identify which neighborhoods to include on our tour.

"From your description, I'd certainly feel at home in Kendall," I said,"but what about you, Betty? Would you be comfortable living in a primarily Latino neighborhood?"

"I guess I'm comfortable with whatever we can afford," she said glumly, picking at her cuticles. "So if that's what it takes to avoid drugs and guns, then that's what it takes." Rosa looked up from the map and raised an eyebrow in my direction. "Besides," Betty added, "I'd welcome the chance to learn more about Latin culture."

"I bet you would," I said, matching her sarcasm exactly. "Are you going to fry me up some coxinhas like a good wife should?"

"Doubtful," Betty said, "but at least we can count on your good cooking if mine fails."

Luckily, it didn't take us long to find a place we could agree on. A modest three-bedroom house with a covered carport and a small fenced-in back yard. Plenty of space for us both and an office as well. I immediately began drawing up a landscaping plan—Del Mar grass, banks of ferns and asters, and an elaborate flower garden. I sat on my back steps, glass of scotch balanced on one knee, cigarette dangling from the corner of my mouth. I exhaled contentedly. Life was going to be good.

Considering we'd come from a two-bedroom apartment, this new home had more than enough room for everything we owned, all of which we'd hauled with us to Miami. We'd driven both cars down from Minnesota—my VW bug and Betty's Ford Taurus, to which we'd hitched a trailer loaded with our combined furniture and household goods.

Thanks to her transfer from St. Paul, Betty was able to start working as soon as we were settled into the new house. She kept long hours during those first weeks. It was important to her to get oriented and establish herself as quickly as possible. Not wanting to freeload for long, and with Betty's diligence to galvanize me, I began my own job search. Construction was still booming in Miami, thanks to the fast-flowing drug money and the serious problem of laundering it. Dumping cash was treacherous and the solution of choice in the early 1990s was real estate. Knowing this, I focused on construction jobs and found one almost instantly.

Soon I was working even longer hours than Betty. But that didn't stop me from getting out and meeting our new neighbors. I introduced myself to every single neighbor I saw. Within the first week, everyone on the block was greeting me by name and along with the greetings came invitations to cookouts and poker parties. All of this was much to Betty's dismay. "It's a lot, Bruno," she said when I told her about three different get-togethers we could hit up that evening. "We just got here, I'm working hellishly long days, and—."

"I understand, I do," I cut in, "but I'm still going to get you out into the neighborhood this weekend, even if I have to carry you on my back. These people are friendly, Betty. You'll see. And I promise to stay right by your side the whole time. I cross my heart." I made the sign of the cross over my chest, that time-tested proof of good intentions. It worked, because that Saturday Betty and I attended our first neighborhood event: an afternoon backyard barbecue.

One little issue I hadn't considered was that the first language of most of the guests at the party was Spanish or Portuguese, and only a few of them spoke English. This put Betty in quite a predicament. Since our marriage she had picked up a few Portuguese phrases, but she was in no way prepared for the rapid-fire conversations shooting off in all directions. Her lips drew tighter and she looked more foul every time I glanced her way. I tried to translate enough of what was said to make her feel more comfortable while simultaneously engaging with the fray myself—but it was no easy feat. Granted, I love to talk, but even I found it difficult to keep up with four or five conversations, in three different languages, all at the same time. Especially given how many shots of scotch I had pulsing through my veins. The hosts had placed the bottle I'd brought them as a gift on the drinks table, and without intending to, I'd made quite a dent. By the time the ribs were being dished up, succulent and aromatic, swimming in a deep, tangy sauce, Betty was fed up. She leaned toward me and whispered loudly, "I'm out of here, Bruno."

"Don't be silly. I'll go with you." I didn't bother to whisper since no one was listening to us anyway.

"Forget it," she snapped. "You'd obviously rather stay. Just make an excuse for me and I'll get out of your hair." I tried to assess her sincerity, unsure whether she genuinely wanted me to stay and enjoy myself, or whether it was just my scotch-colored glasses making it seem that way. Clearly she was annoyed, that much was certain, but was she going to be even angrier later if I let her leave alone? Before I could formulate my reply, Betty walked away, leaving her untouched plate of food steaming on the porch rail beside mine.

I might have ended up chasing after her had I not looked across the yard and seen, looking directly at me, the same guy who'd been watching me for the last two hours. All evening this guy had been stealing looks in my direction. Maybe it was the booze, maybe it was the electric atmosphere of Miami itself, but when he looked my way, I felt more alive than I had in a long, long time. I walked over and held out my hand. "Hey," I said. "I'm Bruno. I don't think we've met yet. I just moved into the neighborhood two weeks ago with my wife, Betty—she left just a moment ago, her allergies are acting up. Anyway, we're in the little yellow house four doors down."

"Anthony, Anthony Nunez." He shook my hand, holding my gaze steadily. The touch of his palm to mine was shockingly intimate. Looking into his intense brown eyes, almost black, I got the same feeling I had as a boy when, while wading into the ocean, I stepped over the edge of a sudden drop off. In spite of myself, I looked away. "How do you like Miami so far?" Anthony asked. A conversational flotation device.

"Better and better every day," I said, beginning to regain my bearings. "Have you lived here long yourself?"

The disorientation persisted, definitely made worse by all that scotch—I knew I was drunker than I should be, and yet, that didn't stop me from accepting his offer to get us both beers from the cooler. When eye contact became too overwhelming, I took a deep drink. I committed each fact I learned about Anthony to memory: he was from Venezuela, he owed his near perfect English to his upbringing in a "government" family and a year spent in California as a high school exchange student. He had arrived in Miami in May, two months earlier. I saw an opening.

"You must be pretty familiar with this area by now," I said. "More familiar than I am, at least. Would you mind showing me around a bit? You know, let me in on the little insider secrets like the café to go to for a good espresso, that kind of thing. Maybe tomorrow, if you have time?" I threw back the rest of my beer.

"I'm free all day. When and where?"

We arranged to meet after lunch at the local soccer field. I left the party soon after we'd agreed on the plan. The combination of all that scotch, beer, sun, and Anthony had me drunker than I'd been in a while. It probably didn't help that I had been so caught up in the conversation that I hadn't eaten even a single rib—mine or Betty's! When I reached our house, I flopped down on the grass in the front yard, nauseous but happy. The grass felt cool against my skin. I lay back and watched the faraway lights in the sky above me spin over my head. I lit a cigarette and lingered.

CHAPTER SEVEN

A Little Samba

By 7 a.m. the next morning, I was already showered, dressed, and halfway through a pot of dark coffee. Not that I needed any more nervous energy than was already coursing through my veins. I'd hardly slept at all—I awakened every hour, on the hour, all through the night—and yet, I felt more awake and alert than I had in weeks. It was like when I'd first arrived in the United States from Brazil, when my senses were so on fire, so attuned to every sight, sound, and smell. All I could think of was Anthony.

I moved around the steamy kitchen as quietly as I could so as not to disturb Betty, who was still out cold in her room. I wanted to sweeten her mood after last night and surprise her with breakfast in bed. Morning sun lit up the eastern window over the sink, and according to the thermometer that hung beside the window, it was already 90 degrees outside. I wiped sweat from my forehead with a paper napkin. In the cast iron pan I had two eggs—Betty liked them over easy—and two strips of bacon, sizzling and curling. The bacon was approaching peak crispness, so I put the English muffins into the toaster and poured the V-8 vegetable juice into a tumbler. Betty loved English muffins and V-8.

I whistled as I worked, quietly at first, but I soon forgot myself and sang out loud, dancing between the refrigerator and the stovetop. The bathroom door opened and closed. Betty must have heard that last verse of "Uma Nota So." That was OK, though. Perfect timing actually, because everything was ready. All I had to do was spread the butter on the English muffin, making sure it melted down into every little crevice. I wanted everything to be exactly right. I angled one half of the muffin slightly atop the other and then assessed the tray one last time. It needed something. I opened the refrigerator and grabbed some parsley from the crisper, tore off a few sprigs, then stuck them in the tumbler of V-8. "Perfect," I whispered to myself. I carried the tray to Betty's bedroom and set it on her dresser so that I could smooth the bedclothes before setting the tray down for her. I heard the toilet flush, then the faucet running. Moments passed. Impatient, I knocked lightly on the bathroom door.

"What in the world?" Betty swung the door open, flustered by my intrusion.

"Good morning *meu amor*. I'm your servant today and I've started out with your breakfast, which is getting cold. If it pleases Your Highness, may I suggest you cut short your primping and return to your bedroom where your breakfast awaits?" I beamed at her.

Betty laughed. "I was hardly primping," she said, turning back to the mirror and holding a thatch of her brown hair near her face, so the ends fell just above her chin. "It's just that—well, to be honest, I was thinking about what Rosa said the other day, about how I should cut my hair short. Even if she's right about it flattering my face, I wouldn't know how to style it. I mean, how long do you think it takes her to get ready each morning?" With that, Betty pulled the rest of her hair back, gave her reflection one last stare, and turned to face me. "Anyway, I've never had breakfast in bed, not ever," she said. "I don't know how bacon and eggs taste in the bedroom."

"I haven't either," I laughed, "but I hear it's delicious."

As Betty brushed past me, I couldn't help but feel a wave of pity to think of her comparing herself to my sister. Impossible. Rosa had inherited my mother's uncanny beauty. Her features, somehow both delicate and strong, gave her face the captivating quality of a classic movie star. I also happened to know that Rosa's daily beauty routine took less than ten minutes—her beauty was natural through and through. But man, if my sister felt like getting dolled up, she had the skills to paint her face and style her hair however she chose. Betty could get the most flattering hair cut in the world, I thought, watching her settle her broad frame against her pillows, but she could never, ever hold a candle to my sister.

"Dig in," I said to Betty, setting the tray on the bed beside her, "before your yolks lose their runniness." I turned toward the door.

"Wait, aren't you going to eat with me?" she asked.

"I made this all for you," I said. "You enjoy yourself. I'll be in the kitchen cleaning up for my queen." The truth was that there was no way I could sit still next to Betty. It would be torture, a physical impossibility. All I could think of was Anthony. All I wanted was to be alone with my thoughts, in my dizzy, intoxicated state of longing.

As soon as I finished tidying the kitchen, I went out to the garden to continue my work on the southwest corner, where I was installing a vegetable patch. I was building a raised bed for the tomatoes, peppers, and herbs. Two-by-eight pine planks on all four sides would contain the soil. By now, the day was growing unbearably hot. I went back to the house for a bandana to tie around my head. The shower was running; Betty's tray sat empty on the kitchen counter. She had washed her dishes and stacked them neatly in the drainer to dry. So much for my being her servant. I went back to the garden, belting out, "This is just a little samba, built upon a single note . . . ."

Soon I had the entire perimeter of the raised bed solidly constructed. I was just about to head in to refill my glass when Betty came out the back door. "What are you singing?" she wanted to know. "You were singing that same song earlier."

"Must be stuck in my head," I said. "It's a popular song from my wild teenage years. Oldie but goodie." Now, I decided, was as good a time as any to broach the difficult topic of Anthony. Waiting would only make it worse. Worse for me, at least. Because the awkward guilt I felt over saying nothing was becoming unbearable, and I hadn't even met with him alone yet.

"Hey, Betty, you know that guy who kept staring at us at the party yesterday?"

She looked blank. "What guy?"

"The good-looking one," I said.

"How about a little more detail?"

"Not as short as me, but not tall, maybe five feet ten. Dark hair, dark eyes. Smoldering attitude."

"Give me a break," Betty said. "There were dozens of people there, none of them speaking English, the entire yard was a sweathouse, and I'm supposed to remember a good-looking guy with a smoldering attitude?" Even in simply recollecting the afternoon, Betty's face turned dark. Then something—a flash of recognition—flickered in her eyes. She shielded her face against the sun and stared intently at the planks I'd just put in place. Then she looked at me again. "Why do you ask, anyway?"

"It's just I talked to him after you left," I said. "He's from Venezuela. I'm going to meet him this afternoon so he can show me around this neighborhood and some parts of Miami he likes."

"So that's what's behind your manic mood," she said, "and your so-called breakfast in bed. You feel guilty because you have a date."

"Come on, Betty," I protested. "It's not a date. I don't even know for sure that he's interested in men, or in me, other than as a fellow South American and neighbor."

Betty stared at the vegetable garden behind me for a minute, then she turned all the way around to the side garden, where I had installed a curved brick path lined with marigolds. "Don't think I'm going to try to stop you," she said, "because I'm not. I have more dignity than that. But don't kid yourself, Bruno. Some bacon and eggs in bed doesn't give you the right to have a boyfriend and expect me to like it. Because I don't." She turned and stomped toward the house.

Suddenly I was embarrassed to think that I had actually hoped to ask Betty for advice about how to best handle the meeting with Anthony. Clearly that wasn't going to be possible! I thought about following her into the house, but decided against it. Better not to get her more riled up than she already was. Besides, all I really wanted to think about was Anthony. I honestly did not know his intentions, but our conversation had felt flirtatious. It was so hard to be sure. I was rusty. It had been a long time.

The soccer field was just a few minutes walk and so, not wanting to be too early, I took an indirect route. Anthony was standing near the goalposts when I arrived, wearing form-fitting jeans and a brightly colored Tommy Bahama short-sleeved shirt. I couldn't help but stare. My pulse throbbed in my ears.

Anthony waved, the muscles in his forearm and bicep tensing and flexing. "Bruno! Right on time! I just got here two minutes ago."

"Hey, man, thanks for doing this," I said. "You lead the way and I'll follow."

"So yesterday you mentioned espresso," Anthony said. "The place to go is Overflow. The shots they pull will kick your ass. In a good way." He grinned. "It's just a few blocks that way." He pointed eastward and started walking.

We found a table in the back of the café, next to a window. "You have to try their guava pastelitos," Anthony said. "Trust me on this."

While we waited for our coffees and pastry, I found myself staring again. The lines of his jaw were utterly mesmerizing. I forced myself to look out the window instead. "This is a great neighborhood," I said. "How did you end up here? Tell me your story, Anthony Nunez." I savored the feel of his name on my tongue.

"It's long. And boring."

"I doubt it."

The barista approached our table with our coffees. She had piercings up and down both ears, in her lower lip, and through her septum. She was also heavily tattooed all over her body, an intricate map of color and form covering the bare skin her tank top and cut-off shorts put on display. The tattoo on her forearm read Namaste. I was grateful for a visual distraction; already I felt I was letting my eyes linger too long on Anthony. I stirred sugar into my coffee and then spoke in the most casual tone I could muster. "Believe me," I said, "there's no way your story can bore me, no matter how long it is. I want to know everything about you."

"Everything?" Anthony raised the white porcelain cup to his lips then set it back down again abruptly, spilling some of the liquid onto the Formica table. "Hot!" he said. "Way too hot!"

Our eyes locked.

"OK, so maybe by the time the coffee cools, I'll have given you all the highlights of my life so far." He tore a flaky piece off the top of his pastry. "The facts are predictable enough, I guess. You'll probably know the ending before I get there."

"Try me."

"My parents are from the upper class in Venezuela. Dad's a politician—and our family name, Nunez, is well recognized and widely respected in Venezuela. So that status, and on the flipside, the specter of losing it, came into play six months ago when I noticed I wasn't feeling great and went to our family doctor. He discovered that I'm HIV positive." Here, he tried the coffee again, bringing it near his lips but not to them before setting it back down in vain.

"Our doctor told my father immediately. Can't blame him, really. Dad has a lot of clout. My parents didn't know I was gay, of course. So Dad's first thought was for his reputation. Hell, his only thought was for his reputation. In Venezuela, and especially in his circle, it's out of the question to be gay—and it's absolutely unthinkable to be HIV positive. He swore the doctor to secrecy and told me he'd 'make arrangements' to handle the problem."

"Arrangements, like what?"

Anthony held up his palms and swept his gaze around the room. "This. This was his arrangement—a condominium in Miami, a plane ticket, and a fast goodbye. He sends me all the money I need. The only stipulation is that I not contact anyone back home—not friends or relatives. I'm to live my life far away from Venezuela and everyone and everything I used to love."

No wonder his eyes were so sad. "Your mother, what about her?" I asked. "Does she agree with your dad?"

Anthony's face hardened. "My mother would never disagree with my father. But when I kissed her goodbye, she couldn't hold back her tears. She told me she loved me and that I would always be welcome to see her. She does not disown me. It's a distinction in words only. If I contact her without my father's permission, I risk being cut off entirely."

Reflexively, I took hold of his hand. "You probably know this already—that I'm also gay. And I'm HIV positive, too. I found out less than a year ago, when I applied for the green card— the blood test."

He nodded.

"My family hasn't disowned me. Not yet, anyway. Thank God. But then again, only my father knows. He made me promise to keep it secret from my mom. All of it. Being gay, HIV, the whole thing. I didn't realize until he did how bad . . . ."

Anthony pulled his hand away from mine and ran it through his dark hair. "Hold up," he said. "I'm the last to judge anyone for being positive, and I won't deny that I've been flirting with you, but I assumed you were living deep in the closet. If you're out, to your father at least, what about your wife? That was your wife, right? The woman who was with you at the barbecue? If your dad knows you're gay, why would you . . . ."

"Betty," I said. "Yes, it's a strange situation, and a lucky one. She works for Immigration and Naturalization, so that's how I first met her, back in Minnesota. She was so shy—maybe you picked up on that—but once I got her talking, we just hit it off as friends. Then when my blood tests came back, she proposed to me so that I could stay in the country."

"And you never told her?"

"No! I mean, yes, she knows I'm gay. She knew when she asked me to marry her."

"That's extraordinary," Anthony said. "I don't want to be forward, but do you think she's in love with you?"

"I choose to believe her when she tells me she has no expectation of a traditional man-and-wife kind of marriage," I said. "But yes, I do think she loves me. And I love her, too, in a certain way. We have a whole different kind of partnership, where we both get some of what we need."

Anthony stared at me—hard—then lowered his head. He placed his hand slowly on top of mine. The touch of his skin to mine sent a shiver jolting through me." Some? What else do you need, Bruno?"

Before I could form a reply, he pointed out the plate glass window. "See that low white stucco building, to the left? That's where I live."

We paid for the coffee and pastry then walked out of the café, matching each other's pace stride for stride. I felt exposed, like I was missing a few layers of skin.

Anthony unlocked the security gate of his building. The lobby was empty. On the far side was the elevator, its gold metal doors gleaming and beckoning. Anthony pushed the call button. The trip to the fourth floor took hours. I shoved my shaking hands into my pockets. Anthony slowly unlocked the door to his apartment—number 402—and stepped aside to let me enter.

As soon as he closed the door, I pushed him against it, pressing my mouth to his. He pressed his hand to the small of my back and pulled me into him. I ran my hands over his body, savoring the feel of his shoulders, his stomach, his thighs. With one hand, I unzipped his jeans, the other hand already tugging them down and his briefs with them. For a moment I marveled at whatever it was, muscle memory or instinct, that made this feel so easy. His jeans reached his ankles, he kicked them away impatiently. He was naked from the waist down, and nothing else mattered.

When I awoke, the room was pitch dark. If my head hadn't been resting on Anthony's outstretched arm, I would have been certain I had dreamed it all. I stood up as softly as possible, retrieved my clothes—which were scattered helter-skelter down the hall—and dressed myself as quietly as I could. I opened the door soundlessly and shut it just as soundlessly behind myself. Then I headed back home, crawled back into my own bed, and went back to sleep.

When I woke again, late summer sun glared through the window behind the bed. The weather was in perfect keeping with my emotions. I pulled the covers over my head and rolled over, determined to stave off the reality of the day just a little bit longer, desperate to linger in the cocoon of my bed where I could pretend not to know whether the night before was a scintillating dream or a far more scintillating reality. Electric currents crisscrossed my skin. My smallest movements brought back memories of Anthony. Everything around me was realer than real and at the same time, utterly unreal.

I could have stayed in that sweet limbo forever, except that work awaited. Today we'd be framing, the part of the building process that I loved best. I liked the precision that operating the nail gun required, but more than that, I liked the idea that the boards I nailed would become the bones of a lasting structure, and that I was integral to the process of its construction. Soon the 8:45 a.m. bus would be pulling up at the corner, just like always, whether or not I was waiting there to board it. Slowly, painfully, I pushed back the covers and swung my feet down to the tile floor.

The day went by surprisingly fast, filled as it was with nothing but thoughts of Anthony. Even hard work in the hot sun couldn't dissipate the delicious, loose feeling that lingers in the body after that kind of night. Though I had been out of circulation lately, I had enjoyed more than my share of one-night stands before being diagnosed with HIV. Anthony, I knew, could be just another flash of lightning—thrilling, finite, and soon forgotten. In which case I'd hardly need to tell Betty. But what if it was more? It was silly, I knew, to let myself daydream. I had no reason at all to believe that Anthony wanted anything from me other than what he had already gotten. I reminded myself of this fact over and over as I gathered my tools for the bus ride home.

On its way to my stop, the bus passed Anthony's apartment building; its low stucco profile spanned almost three quarters of the block. My heart sped up and I suddenly found it impossible to take a full breath. I was nervous and excited at the mere sight of the building! A rush of warmth spread through my whole body and the yearning to see Anthony became so intense, so physical, that I had to turn away from the window to collect myself.

When I arrived home, the house was empty and quiet. I put some

Manfredo Fest on the stereo. His upbeat music always conjured warm thoughts of Anna and Jim. Manfredo was a great friend of theirs, along with his wife Lili and son Phillip. As a matter of fact, Jim—in his usual generous and spontaneous way—had bought a Yamaha grand piano just so Manfredo would have a proper instrument to play when he came to visit them, which he did often.

I started making dinner and decided to make enough for Betty too, although I wasn't sure how late she planned to work. We hadn't seen each other since our tense conversation in the backyard the previous morning. I poured myself a generous dose of scotch while I stared at the contents of the refrigerator and started pulling things out: four lemons, the shrimp I'd gotten at the fish market on Saturday, red peppers, and a fragrant bunch of cilantro. I whistled along to "Jungle Cat" as I turned to scour the cupboards. This would be fun. First I mixed up a lemon juice marinade for the shrimp with a sprinkle of cayenne. Then I placed that dish in the refrigerator to chill. While I waited for the shrimp to soak in the flavor, I chopped and sautéed an onion and several bell peppers, then added another dash of cayenne, cilantro, and some tomato purée. Once I had finished my first scotch, and poured another few fingers, it was time to stir coconut milk into the shrimp mixture. Then, the finishing touch: dendê oil, the vibrant, orange-red oil that brings to the cooking of my homeland what drums bring to samba.

When the stew was finished, I took my bowl and a fresh tumbler of scotch to the dining room. As I ate I allowed myself to relive the night before, one dangerous, tempting image after the next. Bowl empty, sudden exhaustion hit. The giddiness of the night before had finally drained away, leaving me as spent and empty as an airless balloon. The only thing I could do was to surrender to the heaviness of sleep. I brought my bowl to the kitchen, washed it in the sink, and then divided the remainder of the stew into a Tupperware container and a bowl for Betty, which I covered with plastic wrap. I made sure to place the bowl on the top shelf of the refrigerator so she would see it when she returned home. For now, I was grateful not to have seen her. I didn't want to answer any more questions. At least not now, not yet.

The week sped by in a blur of anxious longing and constant distraction. I just wanted to hear Anthony's voice. But my workdays were so long that I was never alone in the house, and it seemed inappropriate to call him while Betty was home. Although on this point I wasn't entirely certain. She was nothing but cheerful when I saw her Tuesday morning. To my great relief, and almost equally great confusion, she had not even hinted at the topic of Anthony. Perhaps, I thought, she's assuming he turned out to be just a friendly guy willing to show a newcomer around the neighborhood. Or that I made a pass and he turned me down, and she doesn't want to throw salt on the wound. Whatever she thought, it seemed unlikely he appeared in her thoughts as frequently as he did in mine. Yet I didn't call. And if I was being totally truthful, the number one reason was that I was scared—shit scared. I didn't want to come across as desperate, or worse, delusional. If Anthony wanted to hear from me, he had my number.

Finally on Thursday night, as I sat at the kitchen table nursing a third glass of scotch and one of the last cigarettes in my pack, waiting for Betty to get home from work, the phone rang. I knew it was him. My body knew. I sipped once more on my scotch and let it ring again. On the third ring, I picked up the receiver and leaned against the wall.

"Hello?" I tried to sound relaxed and natural.

"Hey stranger. No note, no call?"

My breath caught in my throat. I could barely croak out the words. "I wanted to! I've been crazy busy at work, and things here are, well, things here are complicated." I cleared my throat. "And—I wasn't sure you wanted to hear from me."

"After last Sunday? Don't be an idiot. You don't work on weekends, do you?"

CHAPTER EIGHT

The Feeling of Falling

If I had to pick a favorite feeling out of all the feelings a person can possibly feel, it would have to be the addictive, world-conquering feeling of falling unexpectedly and rapidly in love. And no place could be a better setting for that feeling than the mania and magic of Miami in those years. I fell for neon-lit South Beach almost as hard as I fell for Anthony. Everything there was frenzied in the best of ways. The foam parties that left you neck-deep in bubbles, your bare torso pressed against the equally bare bodies next to you. Never had I seen the kind of fearless, public flirtation (and more) that took place in Flamingo Park. But lurking just under that sparkling, pastel surface was a retributive ugliness. Beer bottles and nasty slurs sliced through the throbbing, late night air.

Anthony appreciated the freedom of the scene, especially in the least public spaces. The true VIP rooms, where velvet ropes are superfluous because the only ones who know how to find them are already on the list. But he always gave the impression that he would have been equally happy to hole up with me in his apartment. I, on the other hand, was drawn to the action like a light-starved moth to a flame. Weekdays blurred together as if I had pressed fast-forward on a videocassette, speeding me toward the weekend.

Betty griped about my being out every Friday and Saturday night, but then again, what didn't Betty gripe about these days? I shared vague, abbreviated stories with her about my nights on the town. I mentioned Anthony's name as little as possible, though it was constantly on the tip of my tongue. Once in a while she'd ask outright where I was going and who I was meeting. Sometimes I told her. Sometimes I didn't. "Well," she said tightly, "I hope you can pull yourself together soon, Bruno. The house is starting to look like a shambles." It was an exaggeration, but also partly true. The things I had devoted myself to before—gardening, devising elaborate recipes—now received only droplets of my diverted attention. My raised vegetable garden got choked out with untended weeds. And you know what? I didn't care a bit.

Then one Friday night in November, Anthony cancelled our plans at the last minute. Worse yet, he did it by leaving a message on our answering machine. I was shocked. This would be the first Friday night we had spent apart since we left that café together. Anthony offered no explanation, and I didn't want to call him back with Betty in the room. This definitely wasn't the kind of conversation I wanted to have in her earshot. The cancellation sunk me into a black mood, especially since Anthony had left the club where we'd been partying together early—and now that I thought about it, rather suddenly—the Friday before.

Late Friday night (or, to be more accurate, in the wee hours of Saturday morning), when too little sleep and too much alcohol had fuzzed my brain past the point of caution, I made my way to Anthony's apartment. A murky, dark part of me wondered if I would find him with someone else. To my relief, when I let myself into his apartment with the spare key he kept on the slim ridge of the door frame, I found him alone and fast asleep. He didn't even stir when I crawled into bed beside him. I was high off more than just the hours of wild dancing, and I couldn't resist the feel of his skin. I tried to rouse him twice, but both times he rolled away, the last time with a growled, "Stop." So I let myself pass out. And when I awoke around noon, he was gone.

After another scotch-soaked whirl though South Beach, I ended Saturday night in my own bed, which now felt sterile and unfamiliar. I woke early on Sunday with a stark feeling of panic. Something was really wrong. I wanted to call but had to find the right words, the right apology. I could fix this if I treaded carefully. I had to fix this. But before I gathered my courage, he called me. "I need to see you," he said. "At the café. How soon can you be there?"

"I'm on my way."

I arrived first and was glad for the chance to settle into a booth and collect myself. I didn't want to look as keyed up as I felt. Once Anthony arrived, though, it was hopeless. The attraction mixed with dread was so overpowering that it sucked up all the air. For the first time, annoyance eddied in the void. We had so little time to give to each other, and he had robbed us of a whole weekend together.

Finally he broke the silence. "The last five years in Venezuela, I attended too many funerals," he said, without setting down his cup and without moving his eyes from the table. "I've lost almost a dozen friends to AIDS. I don't—I can't go through it again. I won't,

Bruno. Whatever this is, this thing between us, I can't stand by and watch you dance while a death sentence dangles over your head."

"So you're ending it? Because I have HIV?" I would have been less surprised to hear he had taken up with a woman.

"No, Bruno, not because you have HIV. Because you're living like a man with nothing to lose, like any day could be your last, and you don't give a shit about what that does to you or anyone else."

"You're damn right I have nothing to lose, and any day could be my last. I could develop full-blown AIDS any second. So could you. So could anyone with HIV. The doctor said I might get ten years, if I'm lucky. I'm going to make the most of them. And for that, you're cutting me out? That is unbelievably unfair. You of all people!"

"You're wrong, Bruno, and so was that doctor. Simply and completely wrong. And yes, I of all people do know better. New treatments are being discovered all the time. Have you heard of Hivid? Maybe as ddC?" He barely paused, already sure of my answer. "Yeah, I didn't think so. With the latest treatments, they can even help people with drug-resistant strains. HIV isn't a death sentence anymore. If you gave a shit about yourself, you'd know that."

"I see how it is," I said coldly. "You want me to sit at home checking my pulse and rushing to the refrigerator to count out my pills? Choke down some crackers that I know I'll vomit right back up? Maybe I don't know about that dd-whatever, but I've seen what treatment does. I'd rather take my chances and enjoy myself in the meantime."

"Well, well, is anyone here surprised?" He looked around the café and raised his palms in the direction of the three other patrons who were quietly sipping coffees or eating pastries. I found myself wishing we'd chosen a busier café. "How quaint that you're turning down drugs, now, Bruno. That's a first. But you'll keep drinking scotch like water, I assume? A cigarette constantly between your lips? You're literally poisoning yourself—."

"When life is so short—."

Anthony slid out from the booth and stood up. He looked lean and strong and absolutely furious. "Don't you dare tell me about how short life is, as if you have no choice in the matter."

He put his hand up to stop me from the retort that was already spilling out of my mouth.

"Don't," he said. "Just don't. I plan to live a long, long life. A full life. I take care of myself. I'm setting myself up for a fabulous fucking future."

"Well, how amazing for you, Anthony. So if you have such a perfect little plan, then tell me this, why did you talk to me at that barbecue? Take me home? Screw me? Why do I know where you hide your key? Credo, Anthony, if my lifestyle upsets you so much, why let this . . . whatever this thing is between us . . . go so far?"

"Because I want—I want more, that's what I want, and I want you to want more, too. Not this, not you stumbling back to me at daybreak soaked in foam and whatever the hell else—."

"If you think there's some other guy—."

"I'd rather there was some other guy than just this death-wish attitude, this selfish indulgence in every form of self-destruction out there. God, Bruno, you could have such a good life if you just took your head out of your ass long enough to make it happen."

Two young mothers with toddlers in strollers had just pushed their way through the café doors, laughing, when our shouting erupted. They stopped to stare, ready to back out the door if a fistfight ensued. But there would be no fistfight.

We stared at each other across the table. I watched his ribcage rise and fall with each breath he took. Finally he gave his head a quick, hard shake, threw a wad of dollar bills onto the table, and walked out the door. The day had grown windy, and the chimes above the café door jangled as he exited. I followed him out the door then turned west, into the glare of the late afternoon sun. Every cell in my body wanted to look back over my shoulder, but I refused to let myself. Just one glance. Just to see if he was looking, too. I was still too proud, too stubborn. I was walking away.

The street swam before my eyes—pedestrians hurrying along in pairs and trios, dishwashers and bus boys on smoke breaks outside sidewalk cafés, open storefronts flanked by stands of cheap trinkets, vendors selling tamales and shaved ice—it all melded into a liquid mix of colors, smells, sounds. The wind blew stronger, and despite the sun burning in the clear sky, I felt cold cut all the way through me for the first time since moving to Miami.

As I walked on, I thought of Anna and Jim and their light-filled sunroom overlooking Lake Minnetonka. I thought of the last time I spoke with my father, in that same sunroom, the curl of smoke from his cigarette backlit in the slant of evening sun, the painful promise he'd bound me to over empty Champagne flutes and an overflowing ashtray. I thought of the note of joy in my mother's voice when she greeted Betty—"My new daughter," she had exclaimed. Betty, who had so unexpectedly become the person who made the life I was living in the United States possible. And how did I repay her? By sneaking around behind her back. I'd turned us into some twisted, bizarro version of that tired, old, cheating husband/steadfast wife stereotype.

I walked faster and faster, walked and walked and walked, past my own street, past any familiar landmarks, past the distant edges of the neighborhoods I knew. I walked until I lost track of how many blocks I had gone. I walked until I had no idea where I was.

When I finally arrived back home, Betty was sitting on the beige living room couch, *People* magazine spread open on her lap, a cup of tea in her hand. Her face was bare, her hair pulled back tight. "Bruno?" she said. Her eyes were wide open, her shoulders and neck taut. She looked like she was about to snap.

"Oh, Betty!" I said, and threw myself onto my knees in front of her. I knew I was being dramatic, but I couldn't help it. "I've made such a mess. I fucked up everything, Betty. Everything. And I'm sorry for that. Just say you believe in me, and I can do anything. I promise."

"What are you talking about?" Even as she asked the question, she glowered at me.

"You know exactly what I'm talking about, Betty." Still kneeling, I took the magazine from her lap and the teacup from her hands, and placed both on the coffee table. The smell of Lipton's lemon from her cup was a whiff of comfort on a day gone wrong from the minute I awoke. I took a deep breath.

"First of all, Betty, I owe you an apology for the way I've treated you with regard to—." I found it difficult to say Anthony's name.

Betty scowled. "I don't want—."

"No, let me finish," I interrupted. "This is hard enough as it is. When you asked me to marry you, we never talked about other men. More to the point, I never talked about other men. And I should have. It was foolish of me to leave it to fate, to assume that you would simply understand if and when I met a man. And then I just took up with him, with—Anthony—without saying a word to you. As if it was none of your business. After that first date, which I didn't even call a date, I never even told you when I saw him, let alone asked you how you felt about—."

"As if you couldn't see—."

"Right, of course I could see. Listen, do you know why I didn't raise the issue of other men when you first asked me to marry you? I do. Because I'm a coward. I didn't want to rock the boat. I wanted your kindness, I wanted to stay in the country, and I didn't want to risk losing all those things I wanted so dearly by pointing out what I knew would happen sooner or later. That was so unfair to you. Nossa Senhora, I'm ashamed of myself. I don't know what to do. I don't want to screw things up any more than I already have."

"Can I talk now?"

"Please."

"I knew who you were when I married you, Bruno. You're gorgeous, you're charming, you love people. You love men. I get that. I knew what I was signing up for. But it's true, I'm jealous. I'm not going to lie. Of course I'm jealous! I can't change that. But I didn't marry you to make you into something you're not. I married you so that we could both live our lives on our own terms, somehow. I'm not sure it's possible. But I'm trying."

She crossed her legs on the couch cushion and stared at me. It was me who finally broke the silence. "He sees right through me, Betty. He says I don't care if I live or die. That I'm self-destructive, and selfish, and oh, oh. He says he won't stand for it."

"He shouldn't," she said. "He sees it like it is, your downward spiral. I've seen it for months myself, I just didn't know how to say it."

❧

CHAPTER NINE

Starting Anew

I went to bed that night feeling wrecked. But I woke up the next morning feeling utterly determined. This was it. No more "devil may care" attitude. From now on, I was joining the light side. Anthony's side, whether or not he cared to know I was there with him.

After breakfast I opened the trash bin and threw in a full pack of Marlboros. "Look, Betty. I want you to see this. I'm throwing out my cigarettes," I said. She looked up from the paper and gave me a little smirk. "You'll also be glad to know that I'm taking my full bottle of scotch over to Rosa's and Luigi's this afternoon. I'm off the sauce. Cold turkey."

Now she actually smiled, but only because she didn't believe me. "Sounds like a good start, Bruno. Let's see how long it lasts."

Betty's hair was pulled back loosely at the nape of her neck and the morning light hit her eyes in a way that almost made them glow. My confession had done us both good. "I'm grateful to you, Betty. And I'm going to show you. Or try my best to, at least. I'm cooking up something extra special tonight, something super healthy. Dinner will be a little later than usual, though. Because I'm going to the clinic after work. I want to ask about starting treatment."

A few days later, Rosa called. I was in the throes of a particularly unpleasant headache, just one of the outcomes of my new regimen. Some side effects could be expected, especially in the first weeks of taking the medication, my doctor had said. Headache, nausea, diarrhea. What a picnic. On top of the withdrawal from scotch and cigs and various flavors of club candy, my so-called healthy lifestyle had me feeling like I'd landed on death's doorstep.

"Come to dinner tomorrow night," Rosa said. "You and Betty, both. I want to talk to you." She refused to give me any details over the phone, but she sounded excited. The last thing I wanted to do was to socialize. I felt like the contents of my stomach might be ejected at any moment. When I wasn't caught in the teeth of yet another headache, I was worrying that one might be stalking me, ready to pounce at the least convenient moment. I was exhausted. But I was also determined to be better.

On Thursday evening at 6 p.m., I walked into Rosa's kitchen alone. "I can't, Bruno, how many times do I have to tell you. I have class on Thursday nights," Betty had told me an hour earlier when I reminded her of our dinner plans. "You know that." In fact, I did not. I had a sketchy recollection of Betty telling me her boss had suggested she enroll in an adult learner's Spanish class when we first moved down, but I really hadn't noticed she'd actually done it. Of course, I hadn't noticed much about Betty in recent weeks, to be fair.

"No Betty, Bruno?" Rosa asked as soon as she saw me. "Maybe it's for the best," she continued, before I could explain. "Tonight

can be a family affair. Well, real family. You know what I mean."
Luigi was at the stove as Rosa set the table, and the two girls were
in the backyard with their babysitter. Whatever had gotten Rosa so
worked up must be serious, I thought, for her to have kept the sitter
after hours.

"Betty is family," I said, not wanting to provoke my sister, but
also feeling somewhat loyal to Betty in light of recent events.

"I know Betty's your family, in a way, but she's not . . . ."

That's when he shot out from the hallway to my left, a shocking
blur of color and movement. "Bruno!" My brother had thrown
himself at me so hard and so fast he almost knocked me over.
A wave of nausea and clamminess seized me as I caught myself
and staggered forward, grasping hold of Ricardo as he squeezed
the last drops of air out of me. The nausea mercifully passed in
my brother's embrace. "Bruno! Bruno! Bruno!" he said. "Little
brother! Man, oh man, it's so good to see you, I don't think I can
let go of you!"

"Come on, you two," Rosa said, tugging Ricardo by the sleeve of
his stylish linen blazer. "Sit down! The chicken Alfredo is ready and
we have work to do."

"Hey, I feel tricked," I said. "I thought I was showing up for a
free meal, not a chore list. Don't you think with Ricardo here we
could shelve the chores just for once?"

"Just wait, Bruno," Rosa said as she placed a chicken thigh on my
plate. "You're going to be thanking me in a minute, unless you talk
your way out of the deal."

"Deal?" Suddenly the pieces were fitting together. Ricardo's
unexpected presence, Rosa's heightened bossiness, the nanny
staying late. Something big was in the air—and there was money

involved. "We're starting a new business!" Rosa said, exactly at the moment the thought knitted itself together in my mind. "A state of the art fitness club, even nicer than the one I had in Italy. Ricardo offered to give me all the money I need to get started, and in return, he'll own 49 percent."

"At last, our brother involved in an absolutely legitimate business venture!" I said. "Rosa, you're a miracle worker."

She shot me a look. "I, for one, am beyond grateful for our brother's sales prowess," she said, then returned to the health club as seamlessly as if I'd said nothing. "I'll manage day-to-day operations, of course, and Luigi will handle the financial end. He's licensed for all that, CPA you know, and in Italy he always helped his parents with the finances of their business."

"Keeping it all in the family," I said, smiling to let her know I wasn't going to derail her again.

"Well, that's actually exactly what I have in mind. I've been impressed with you lately. When you dropped off that bottle of scotch, I thought you'd be back to reclaim it within twenty-four hours. Then you hugged me tonight, and for the first time in a long time, you didn't smell like an ashtray someone spilled a drink into."

We all fell apart laughing, then Rosa shushed us. "Seriously, I'm proud of you, probably more than you can really believe or understand." Her eyes looked a little wet. That's one thing I was growing to appreciate about my family, how our love and loyalty seemed to be just about limitless. I thought of Anthony, and the way his parents had turned their backs on him for good. I was starting to realize how lucky I was. "Anyway," Rosa said, "I was thinking you could be a part of the business, too."

"An integral member of the team, in fact," added Ricardo.

"So, what do you say?" Luigi asked. "Are you with us?"

"I love you guys," I said. "And it means so much to know you believe in me. But slow down. Let's not forget that I've got a good job already—a good job, good pay."

"But the opportunity isn't there like it is with this," Rosa said. "Not in the long term. I mean, this is a family business, something you could have a stake in someday. If you wanted that. Your charisma could take us where we need to go—you're our Mr. Personality!"

"I thought that was this guy." I punched Ricardo in the arm.

"Both of you, then, but that's the point," Rosa said. "The more of that secret sauce we've got on our side, the faster we're going to succeed with this. That's why at first I'd want you to man the reception desk and take charge of signing up new clients. But ultimately I'd love your help with planning, design, a little bit of everything. And in the future maybe you could teach a dance aerobics class or two."

All eyes were on me.

"I'm speechless," I said. Then, "Well, almost." I smiled broadly, and the table burst out laughing all over again. "Rosa, you're right about this opportunity. The timing couldn't be better, for so many reasons. So however you think I can help, I'm in."

The next day, I gave notice to my foreman. Rosa's plan was to open by January 1 so we could capitalize on the annual rush of memberships signed in hope of making good on all those unrealistic New Year's resolutions. The timeline was tight, a little over a month, but everyone was committed to pulling it off. Maybe me more than anyone.

Almost two weeks had passed since my meeting with Anthony in the café. Not a word had been exchanged since. The emptiness was unfathomable, so I poured nonstop productivity into it. I woke each morning to his absence. Every choice, from what to have for lunch to endless decisions involved in opening the club, was made with him in mind. The thought of him stayed with me until unconsciousness slid over me at night. It had taken losing him to make me admit I loved him. I would do anything to start again. Hope, fragile yet powerful, had found me.

Other than the lack of snow, Christmastime in Florida was much the same as it had been in the Midwest. Our neighborhood was especially festive thanks to a high concentration of school-children, all of whom exuded contagious excitement over Christmas festivities. Decorated fir trees shone from every window, and carolers stood at every corner. Almost every night featured another neighborhood party. I was working day and night to build up the membership base for the club, but still, I couldn't bear to turn down an invitation. Not for any of the old reasons, but because I was sure I would see Anthony at one of these gatherings. Even if he didn't want to see me. Even if what we had was over for good, unthinkable as that was. If nothing else, I simply wanted to thank him. My turnaround started with him, and if it didn't lead me back to him, he should at least hear from me how right he had been.

For New Year's Eve, we were invited to a party hosted by the same neighbors who had thrown the barbecue where I first met Anthony. And although he had not shown up at a single other neighborhood event, I was sure he would be at this one. But when I arrived, his familiar shape was nowhere in the crush of merrymakers. Disappointed and stone cold sober, I was tempted to cut out and call it a night. Then I thought of Betty.

How inconsiderate that would be, after I had talked her into getting dressed up and accompanying me. So instead of skulking home to feel sorry for myself, I opened a second bottle of Perrier.

"Perrier, not scotch?" He had come up behind me and leaned in close to be heard over the music and the merrymaking. I could feel his breath against my neck.

"Well, then," Betty said abruptly. I opened my mouth to protest, but she shook her head. "I'm off," she said. "You stay. Have some fun for a change. And you," she turned to Anthony, "just look at what you've started. You've helped to save my Bruno's life. Thank you." She paused and gave Anthony a hard look. Then, in an utterly surprising move, she grasped Anthony's cheeks and kissed him on the lips. "Happy New Year," she said. Then she kissed me, too, and Anthony once more, before she motored through the crowded living room and out the door.

"And you said she was shy," Anthony said.

"She usually is! You seem to bring out a whole new side of Betty."

"Mmm," he replied. "How do you think she'll take it when you move in with me?"

"How do I think Betty will take it when I move in with you?" I repeated stupidly.

"Maybe I shouldn't have led with that, considering how things ended the last time I saw you. Let me try again." He rested his chin in his hand and looked me up and down.

"Bruno, you're looking well. Very well. Oh, screw taking it slow, listen, it would make me extremely happy if you agreed to come and live with me at my condo. I'm not asking for a forever commitment. This is not some kind of fairytale or fantasy. I'm just saying, I missed you."

"Anthony." Everything I wanted to say sounded stupid, so I said nothing.

"This past month was miserable," Anthony went on. "I mean, I know you had it worse, the first few weeks of side effects are the hardest though, I promise."

"God, they better be," I said. Then, "Wait, how did you know?"

"Betty tracked down my number. Like I just said, she sure doesn't seem shy. My point is, you're not the only one who's been reflecting and changing and if we're going to do this, let's do it. Together. All the way."

Around the room came a chorus of "Happy New Year!" punctuated by party horns and the metallic banging of pots and pans. Anthony raised his glass of Champagne, and I held my Perrier proudly aloft and clinked it softy against his, superstitions about toasting with water be damned. This was my life, our life, and we could make whatever rules we wanted. Anthony wrapped his arms around me and pulled me into his chest, resting his cheek on the top of my head. I could feel his heart beating. When I opened my mouth to say, "I love you," Anthony was already speaking those words.

CHAPTER TEN

Worlds Collide

I felt high for days after the New Year's party. Every time I closed my eyes I relived it: Anthony's mouth hovering near my ear, his suggestion that we live together, the words "I love you." This high was better than any drug, because my head was clear while all of my senses cross-fired. It was as if the entire world was brighter, louder, sweeter, and more vivid.

When I finally came down to earth, I realized I had to tell Betty what was going on. I expected her to take it hard—the only question was whether she would storm into a rage or break down in tears. I wasn't sure which would be worse. I couldn't stand the anxiety, so the next day I forced myself to get it over with. Betty stood at the sink drying our breakfast dishes, singing along to Paul Simon on the radio. She couldn't carry a tune to save her life and she always got the words wrong, but it was charming the way she tried to belt it out. I watched her until the song ended, then stepped up to the counter beside her. "Betty," I said, "I need to talk to you."

"Help me dry the dishes, then."

"I think it would be better if we sat down."

"I'd rather multitask, but have it your way."

She poured us each a cup of coffee from the carafe on the table. "I bet I know what you're going to tell me," she said. "You're moving in with Anthony." She sipped her coffee and smirked.

I was stunned. "Did he tell you first? He asked me at the party, and I've been thinking it over ever since."

"Thinking it over? Guys like him don't come a dime a dozen."

I couldn't help but laugh. Even if she was being sarcastic, Betty's reaction was catching me off guard in a good way. I had been expecting so much worse.

"Seriously, Betty, before I say anything to Anthony, we need to talk about the lease."

"Maybe you should let me share my news first—I'm getting a raise this month! My supervisor says he's never seen anyone as efficient and talented in my position before. My career is taking off, Bruno—it's moving fast. And with my new salary, I can easily make the payments on my own. And anyway, who knows."

"Who knows what?"

"Who knows what could happen. With me. I mean, it's not entirely out of the question that I could—well, date."

Now she was really taking things in a new direction. I barely knew what to say. "Sure, you could," I said. "You never know what's going to happen next in this crazy life. You could meet a guy at Spanish class. Or at the health club."

"Don't you start in," she said sharply. "I don't need another person getting all over my case about working out more. I hear enough of that from Rosa and frankly, it's getting old fast."

"That's not what I meant," I said. "Not at all. I just—all I'm saying is, you're right, you could meet someone, it could happen anywhere. You're right not to rule it out."

Betty sighed. "Well, that's not even what I'm talking about, anyway. The point is, my job is going places, and I have my own life now. There's no reason for me to fight over you when I have better things to do. I'm not going to get into some kind of petty war with you and Anthony over this."

"A war is the last thing I want," I said. "And don't think I'm leaving you high and dry. This lease is in my name until September 1. That's a commitment I take seriously. Plus, I don't have to pay anything at Anthony's. So I'm paying my share here. No ifs, ands, or buts about it."

"You're not paying anything at Anthony's?"

"Nothing. He's insisting—partly because he understands my commitment to you. Which is more than just financial, Betty."

"If you're leveling with me about not having to pay at Anthony's, then I can accept your paying your half," Betty said. "I'll be able to save for a down payment on my own place, then." She took a sip of her coffee and swallowed. "Bruno, thank you," she said. "Thank you for making good on your financial commitment. I expected you to try to wiggle out of it."

"Never!" I said. "And another thing," I said. "You don't need to worry about the yard. Or that overgrown vegetable garden." Betty laughed harshly. "I'll take care of it just like I used to do. I don't trust anyone else with my garden, anyway. And I'll be right down the street. You can call me day or night. Really."

"I'm plenty competent," Betty said, "as you well know. But if I see one more lizard in this house, I may have to take you up on that offer."

"You got it," I said, raising my coffee cup. "I'm the best lizard chaser I know."

Betty reached for the carafe and poured more steaming coffee into both of our cups. "So when's the big move?"

"Well, your blessing was all I needed, so how about now?"

"But what about packing? I mean—."

"Packing what?" I laughed. "My clothes? My razor and toothbrush? The furniture you can keep." Just then, Prince's "Little Red Corvette" came on the kitchen radio. Betty and I both cracked up.

I stood up to start gathering my clothes into suitcases, and as I packed, the scent of cinnamon filled the house. Betty was apparently baking her signature apple muffins. That reminded me of my mother. I missed both my parents. It had been more than a year since we'd been together.

"Looks like you're all set," Betty said when I dragged my two big suitcases into the living room. She was fumbling through her purse. "I'm heading downtown to meet up with some of the ladies from Spanish class." She pulled out a red lipstick. "You'll be gone before I'm back, so I think this is goodbye."

"Well, let's make it a proper one," I said, opening my arms wide. As soon as Betty opened her arms, I seized her around the waist and lifted her up off her feet, sending her into wails of protest.

"Bruno, put me down!" she shrieked. "My lipstick!" The tube had dropped to the floor and rolled across the rug and beneath the sofa. "Now you actually will need to move this couch," she said. "I want that lipstick back."

Just a few moments after Betty pulled out of the driveway, Anthony and his little red Corvette arrived at the door.

"That's the grand sum of it?" he asked, surveying my pile, one arm wrapped around my waist.

"I travel light."

Anthony had a dresser ready for me, and at least half the space in the bedroom closet. He had even cleared space on all the shelves. "I want this to be our home, yours as much as mine," he said. We made quick work of unpacking, and after we broke down the boxes and put them in the hall, I poked around the kitchen to see about lunch. One peek into his fridge made the options clear. "I think a shopping trip is in order," I said. Anthony suggested a locally owned market six blocks south. Once inside the store I took charge, loading our cart with fruits and vegetables—a bunch of spinach, romaine lettuce, two kinds of mushrooms, avocado, bananas, strawberries and oranges and lemons. Miami offered a cornucopia of fresh food to choose from.

"This is going to work out great for me," Anthony said as I tossed in two garlic bulbs and a mesh bag of Vidalia onions. "I love all this healthy food, but I hate to cook it."

I was thrilled to show off my prowess in the kitchen. I had told Anthony about a few of my favorite dishes, how I used a mixture of Brazilian and French recipes, plus some inventions that were purely my own, but I had never cooked for him. "I had high expectations," he admitted as we sat over our empty plates, stuffed and happy. "But you blew them away entirely. You're an artist. An absolute master. It's a good thing I actually enjoy jogging and working out. Otherwise I'd gain fifteen pounds by next week."

As he said "working out," I realized he didn't even know about my new job at the health club—we had reunited so suddenly, and planned the move so quickly, I had never even brought it up. And now we were in a mad dash to prepare for the grand opening on January 5—just two days away. "There's an opening gala," I told Anthony, after bringing him up to speed, "which is going to take a ton of work on my part. I'm going to be buried these next few days. I may not even have time to sleep."

"I'm excited for you," he said. "Rosa, too."

"And I'm excited for you to finally meet Rosa," I said. "We have so many milestones to look forward to, Anthony. We have so much to be thankful for." I knew I sounded cheesy, but I also knew that Anthony wouldn't think I was cheesy at all—with him, I could never be too sincere. It was a new sensation for me, scary and exhilarating and comforting all at once.

When the big day of the gala arrived, a kind of calm focus overtook me. I watched Rosa throw her head back and laugh at something Anthony said. Betty was just feet away, playing a game of chase with Marlene. She always was more at ease with kids than adults. The more things changed, the more they stayed the same. My separate worlds had come crashing together, and I was at the center of a promising new business. The life unfurling before me looked pretty damn good.

One Saturday morning in February, the phone rang. It was my brother Ricardo, back in Miami after another very exciting jaunt on the yacht with his lady friend—so exciting that he'd extended it and missed our opening. My brother took his cavorting very seriously. "I want to meet that new bride of yours," he said. "Let's get both of you over to my place this weekend. It's already been too long."

"True," I said, as I scrambled mentally to determine the best strategy for appeasing my brother. Obviously I'd have to introduce him to Betty, but it was bound to be awkward. Ricardo was the only one in my family, aside from my mother, who was still unaware of the true nature of my marriage. As soon as we hung up, I picked up the receiver again and dialed Betty's number. Convincing her to come with me to meet Ricardo was quite the task, even more arduous than I expected.

"Bruno, one of the things I like best about our marriage is the independence we've built into it. You have your life, and I have mine. That's the way you wanted it, but you can't have it both ways. Tell your brother whatever you want, but don't expect me to spend my Saturday putting on some charade for you."

"Come on, Betty," I said. "Don't be this way. I know you don't owe me any charades, but I just want the chance to tell my brother the truth about my life one step at a time. All I'm asking for is a few hours of your time so I can introduce my brother to someone important to me."

"So introduce him to Anthony!"

"Oh, for God's sake, Betty." She was staring at me, hard mouthed and jealous. Despite Betty's best efforts at Spanish class and some recent experimenting with a new, shorter hairstyle, she had not been on any dates since I'd moved out. I knew this because Rosa, who was deeply invested in helping Betty make herself over, made sure to keep me up to speed. "Of course I'll introduce my brother to Anthony," I said, "but not yet. First, I would like him to meet you, because you're my wife, and he still believes we're married in the traditional sense of the word. Which you well know! So help me out, this once, for a couple of hours. I'll owe you."

With enough relentless cajoling, bribing, and reminders from me of the important role she played in my life, Betty finally agreed.

I drove over to her place in my bug at 11:30 a.m. the following

Saturday morning and honked at the curb. I was happily surprised at the sight of her when she opened the door: she was wearing a form-fitting shift dress and had tried to pull her new shorter hair back in a loose chignon knot, which didn't look too bad. Betty wasn't anyone's idea of beautiful, but she did have a unique sense of style that was hers alone. I was glad she had carried off a "look" on this particular day, for this particular meeting. "You look great, Betty," I said as she sat down in the passenger seat. "This'll be fun."

"Ha, ha," she scoffed. "Fun isn't the word that comes to mind. Playing the good little wife. Not to mention, from what you and Rosa say about your brother, he sounds quite . . . I don't even know how to say it!"

"You'll love Ricardo," I said. "I mean, it's true, all that about his striking good looks, the whole Hollywood handsome thing, and his razor sharp wit, that's true too. And of course his money. I'm sure he can intimidate when he chooses to, but he's never like that with family. He's a softie, warm and playful as a puppy with big cartoon hearts for eyes. Irresistible. You'll see. I promise."

"Well," Betty said finally, "like you said, I am your wife, and no matter how unusual our marriage is, it does make sense for me to meet your brother. However much of your life you ultimately share with him, it's only logical for you to introduce him to me first, before bringing Anthony into the picture."

"Atta girl!" I said, giving her a soft slug on the arm. "I knew you'd come around eventually." As we sped along Miami's byways toward my brother's estate, the car radio blaring, Betty's tension dissipated slightly. When we pulled onto Ricardo's street, however, her face blanched.

"Wait, I don't—you didn't tell me this," she said. "This is more than I bargained for." A pale brick wall surrounded Ricardo's place with an iron gate guarding the entrance to his long, curvilinear, palm-lined driveway. The opulence was, as I viewed it through Betty's eyes, a little overwhelming, even for Miami high society. "Forget it," she said. "I'm not going to put myself through this after all. Bring me home."

I squeezed her shoulder. "Too late for that," I said. "I'll be by your side the whole time. Besides, you really, really don't want to miss this. Ricardo will wow you, he'll melt you. You may even decide you married the wrong brother." I reached out the open window and pressed the bell at the gate's pillar.

Moments later a short, dark-skinned man wearing a black suit appeared and opened the gate, and we drove into the estate. As I parked to the side of the wide circle drive, evaluating the place through Betty's eyes, I could see how the fountain might be a little much. Her grip on my arm as we walked toward the mansion was uncomfortably tight.

Before I could knock, the front door opened and my brother appeared. His gray linen slacks and short-sleeved white shirt were perfectly tailored to his six-foot-four frame. Fit, muscular, tanned, and relaxed, as always, he looked fantastic. He threw his arms around me in a robust hug that, if it had been any tighter, might have cracked a rib. When he finally let me loose, he turned the shower of uninhibited affection on Betty. I watched as my brother—so tall, dark, and classically handsome, so very different from me—fervently kissed my restrained, Midwestern bride on both cheeks. Growing up, I had never, ever pictured an occurrence like this. "My brother's beautiful new wife!" he exclaimed. "Finally, finally, I meet you in person. Our mother never once stopped talking about you the entire time I was in Brazil. Now I can easily see why. OK, you must both come with me," he said, tucking Betty's hand through his arm. "We have so much catching up to do!"

We followed Ricardo into the foyer with its marble floor and mirrored walls and turned left down a long hallway that led to a series of tall, arched-glass doors. Beyond the glass lay the patio, the pool area, and back gardens. Ricardo rushed to pull out a sling-backed lounge chair for Betty at the umbrella-covered table. His maid arrived as if on cue with a tray bearing a bottle of exquisite scotch. Ricardo poured a few generous fingers in a tumbler and offered it to me. I could smell it even without raising the glass, and my mouth watered with desire.

"Thanks, but no," I said. "Today I'll pass."

"What?" Ricardo protested. "This is Macallan M! I got this scotch especially for you, to celebrate. What now—you want something else? Gin? Rum? Tequila? Name your drink and Gabriella will see to it. Same for the beautiful Betty." Here he turned the full force of his persuasive gaze on Betty, "but if you care for scotch at all, this is a rather nice one."

Gabriella stood patiently, tray balanced midair with seeming weightlessness.

"How about lemonade?" I asked.

"Not acceptable! You must have a proper drink for a proper toast. Mojito? Vodka martini? Bruno, you know I love nothing better than indulging my friends and family. Please don't deny me."

"Tonic water will have to count, then, Ricardo. I'm off booze. Cigarettes too, in fact. I'm squeaky clean these days. But Betty would like a Chardonnay if you have it—wouldn't you Betty?"

Betty arranged her mouth into an awkward smile. "Any white wine, actually," she said. "I'm not fussy."

"Gabriella, a bottle of Chardonnay and," he raised an eyebrow at me, "a tonic water. Twist of lime?" I nodded. "Good." He turned to Betty. "Sister, tell me the truth, is this the real Bruno, or an impostor? Because I'm just not convinced this teetotaler is my brother. As I remember, my brother never turned down a drink in his life, just like our dad. And now he is purer than a priest? Doesn't even smoke? There must be some story behind that." Ricardo beamed his famous smile directly at Betty, that singular smile that made you feel you had known him and loved him forever, and that he adored you best of all, and that you and he were the only two people in the world that would ever matter again.

"Oh, he's the real Bruno, alright," Betty said. "Not to say he hasn't thrown me a few curveballs lately." She rolled her eyes in my direction, her shyness cast aside like a sweater on a sunny day. Her uncharacteristic public teasing would have offered the perfect opening, except that I wasn't actually prepared to talk to Ricardo about Anthony yet. Rosa was one thing, but Ricardo, another. He was so much like my father, a proxy really. I couldn't predict his reaction and I wasn't sure that I wanted to. Definitely not right now.

Gabriella appeared with our drinks, and Ricardo poured himself a second tumbler of Macallan. I must have been eyeing his glass, because he shrugged his shoulders and said, "Somebody's got to drink this bottle, if you won't."

"One sip," I said, taking the tumbler from him and drawing a tiny mouthful. It was an excellent scotch. "Now, we can change the subject for today, and another time, I'll tell you the story, Ricardo. I promise, just not today. For now, let's just enjoy our reunion."

After an hour and a half, Ricardo cut our visit short. "Business," he said. "It makes the world go round. But you're welcome to stay on without me and enjoy the pool and the sunshine."

"Thank you, but we should get on with our day," I said. I had promised Betty we'd stay no longer than two hours at the very most, so this worked well I thought.

"What for?" Betty said. "We have no other plans." Apparently Ricardo's poolside banter combined with two generous glasses of wine had changed the game. Her cheeks were turning a little pink and she looked quite lovely. As I had predicted, despite her apprehensions, Betty had been entranced by Ricardo. He had a kind of magic that all men wanted, that much was absolutely certain. I agreed to stay long enough to enjoy an espresso and a tray of fruit.

Before he made his exit, we arranged another visit in a week. "Same time, same place," he laughed.

"Yes, and I'll be bringing a friend along with me—someone I'd like you to meet," I said.

The following Saturday I took Anthony to Ricardo's mansion. Just as with Betty, it took a ridiculous amount of wheedling to convince him to go with me. "I need you there," I begged. "I'm going to be turning his world—or at least his view of my world—upside down."

"Like he really doesn't know you're gay? Or at least suspect it?"

"Of everyone in my entire family, Ricardo has always been the one I'm most sure has no idea I'm gay," I said. "And now he's going to learn not only that I'm gay, but also that I'm HIV positive, that my marriage to Betty works in a way he won't know how to begin trying to understand if he even wants to, oh, and that I am in love with and living with you. A man. And I'm happier than I have ever been in my life."

Anthony kissed me on the mouth. "For that, I'll go meet your brother. Let's do this."

As soon as we were seated by the pool, at the same table where Betty had gotten tipsy and playful just a week earlier, I clasped Ricardo's shoulder and took the plunge: "I'm ready to tell you my story," I said.

"Finally," Ricardo said. "I've been in agony!"

"First of all—Anthony," I said. I realized I was sweating a little in my navy polo shirt. This was both easier and harder than I'd imagined. "Anthony's more than my friend," I pressed on. "He's my lover. And Betty is my wife. As you know. We have a unique arrangement: I help her and she helps me. It started with my diagnosis. That's the second thing. Or maybe the third. A big one, no matter what. I'm HIV positive, Ricardo."

"No!" He reacted with his entire body, pushing his chair back from the table. I wasn't sure if he was going to leap up and walk away, or hug me, or overturn the table.

"Stay with me, here," I said, pressing my palms into the table.

He gripped the arms of his chair but stayed seated.

"If I don't get this all out at once, I may never get it out at all. So just listen until I'm done. It's not as bad as you might think. Dad knows. I told him back in Minnesota right when I found out, when Betty and I were first married—she offered to marry me because of the diagnosis, knowing that I was gay, knowing that I was sick—and Dad was so much better about it than I feared, except that he made me promise never to tell Mom, he said it would kill her. So I haven't, even though it breaks my heart. But I told Rosa and she's been wonderful, just totally wonderful. Even bringing me in on the health club—and I'm grateful to you for that, more than you know—that job means the world to me, it's part of a bigger picture of the life I'm trying to build. You know I'm not drinking now, not smoking, eating right, and all that's inspired by Anthony. The way I was before, I was running myself into the ground. He saved me, Ricardo, really. Saved my life. For that, at least, I hope you can accept his role in my life. And I hope you can accept me, now that you know."

"You're finished now?" Ricardo asked.

I nodded.

"*Meu irmaozinho,*" he said. "*Meu irmaozinho.*" He whistled through his teeth. "You've been through hell and back. But here's where it begins and ends, little brother: family. Blood. You're my blood, and that's the end of the story. Nothing changes—you hear me? Nothing changes." I looked down at my lemonade to hide the tears behind my eyes.

Anthony took my hand and fixed his gaze on Ricardo. "Everyone should be so lucky as to have a brother like you," he said.

CHAPTER ELEVEN

Beautiful Ordinariness

For the next year, life carried on with a beautiful ordinariness. Even at the height of my honeymoon phase with Anthony, I reserved at least some small part of my attention for Betty. I was committed to upholding my obligations to her. I also had some self-interest in mind. The truth is, I realized early on that it would be ideal for me if Anthony and Betty became friends. The better they liked each other, the less trouble they'd make for me about our unusual arrangement. With that in mind, I made a point of inviting Betty to join us for dinner; some nights she came to our condo after work, other nights we met her at her place. To my surprise, the two of them hit it off better and faster than I had hoped. To my dismay, the reason for this was mostly due to the difficulties they both experienced when dealing with my family.

For Betty, it was friction with Rosa that was constantly sending up sparks. Often, I was the one who got burned—mostly because I didn't keep my mouth shut. I genuinely believed Rosa meant well when she offered Betty suggestions on how to wear her hair, or encouraged her to attend more classes at the fitness center ("at a discounted family rate, of course"). "She's just criticizing me in a backhanded way," Betty would complain. "All of her so-called suggestions are just thinly disguised put-downs." Then whenever I tried to reassure Betty that Rosa actually meant well, my efforts just fanned the flames of her rage even higher.

As for Anthony, he got along with Rosa just fine. Ricardo, however, was another story. Anthony approved of Ricardo's unequivocal acceptance of me—but that was just about the only facet of my brother's character that Anthony didn't question. Whereas Betty had proved extra-susceptible to my charming brother's charms, Anthony appeared entirely immune. When one, or the other, or both of them got going on the faults of my various family members, I took solace in the fact that they were talking to each other without my having to coax the conversation along.

Establishing a friendship between my wife and my lover was just one of the complex tasks I faced. I also had my work at Rosa's fitness center to attend to, where my role seemed to expand by the day. Meanwhile, Anthony enrolled in a few classes at the community college. Though he was still tormented by his father's dismissal, the fat checks that arrived each month made it possible for him to set his schedule however he liked since he had no need to find a paying job. One day, I knew, he hoped to return to Venezuela to work in education.

Despite the hurt that came when he was sent away, Anthony was at heart his father's son, and still deeply invested in current affairs in his homeland. I don't believe he ever seriously considered a career that wasn't somehow connected to public service. Over dinner he'd grouse about rising crime rates and reports of political and economic instability. Finally I admitted, to Anthony's eternal amusement, that I had no real idea who Hugo Chavez was. I barely followed the current events in the United States, let alone in other countries—even Brazil. Anthony was the polar opposite. Even from a distance, he analyzed shifts in policy, explaining to me the probable factors behind each decision. He analyzed it all like an enormous and complicated game of chess. And somehow, still, he staunchly supported the party he had quite literally been raised in.

Anthony didn't speak about his family often. I was curious, but it was his most tender spot so I didn't press. Instead, I bided my time, listened carefully to his political rants and occasional musings, and bit by bit, I learned his history.

He grew up in Campo Alegre, the most exclusive district in Caracas, Venezuela's capital. As children, he and his sister Daniela— she was six years younger than him—hid under tables at the Quinta Esmeralda, where the city's upper class gathered to drink, dance, and negotiate. Weekends were spent at the Caracas Country Club, whose meticulously manicured grounds, designed by the same pair of brothers who planned Central Park, lay in the cool shadow of Mount Avila. Both Anthony and Daniela amassed collections of trophies for golf, swimming, and equestrian shows. "My family," he told me once with a wry smile, "breeds to win." Accomplishments were met with affection, anything else with stony disapproval. Anthony described his mother, Roberta, as a handsome woman with a ringing laugh. When she was alone with him and his sister, she loved to play elaborate games of make-believe. But his father was the final authority on all matters. "He loved us," Anthony said, "but I always knew he loved Venezuela more."

Betty's childhood, in almost every way, couldn't have been more different from Anthony's. By the time she was eight years old, it was rare for her parents to spend more than a week at a time under the same roof with their children. Until she met me, she had never even seen a bottle of Champagne in real life, whereas Anthony grew up drinking Moët & Chandon from Baccarat flutes. The common ground between their starkly different worlds, aside from me, and my forceful family, was academic achievement. I had never been much of a scholar myself—yet another reason I'd been so opposed to the whole college idea back in Minnesota when Anna and Jim had tried to persuade me to enroll. Yes, I felt I was too old, but I also simply lacked the interest and discipline for book learning.

Sometimes, when Betty and Anthony got going on some twisting philosophical tangent, I lapsed into silence and simply admired the scads of information they both housed in their respective brains. Sometimes I wondered if, had they not met me, they might have spent their lives alone with their well-stocked minds. What I lacked in terms of scholastic knowledge, I more than made up for with social expertise. As time passed, the three of us found our strengths and weaknesses, quirks and foibles, fit together to form an awkward whole.

One day—it was near the end of April, 1995, more than a year after I moved in with Anthony—Betty arrived at our condo in an absolute tizzy for one of our regular dinners. She buzzed around the kitchen, too excited to sit down. "Bruno," she said as she pulled the plates and napkins from the cupboard. "This is the best day of my life. Better than our wedding day, if you can imagine that!" She laughed.

Our wedding day had become a kind of running joke between us: the ceremony with no guests, the calamitous luncheon with Anna and Jim afterward, Betty's sweat-soaked red dress.

"What? You won the lottery?" Anthony asked.

"Practically! I'm buying a house!"

"No way! When? How? Where?"

"We demand details," Anthony said. "Starting with a full description of the house."

"Oh, the house, the house!" Betty said. She was as close to gleeful as I'd ever seen her. She took the kale and potatoes from me and carried them to the table. I brought out the plate of seared sea scallops—they were, I congratulated myself silently, perfectly done—and I motioned my wife and my lover to sit down. My wife and my lover! The unusual circumstances of my life never ceased to surprise me.

"Yes, the house, Betty," Anthony said. "The one you're buying."

"Actually, you could both picture it quite accurately without me saying another word." Betty laughed. "You've seen it! Because I live in it! I asked my landlord if he would be interested in selling the house to me, and he said yes."

"Betty, that's fantastic!" I said. "And you can afford it?"

"Thanks to you, I can. That's the beauty of it, Bruno!"

"I'm thrilled for you, but I don't know if I'm following."

"You remember Edna? My friend from Spanish class? Well, she's a realtor and she helped me research the market value. Because of the work you did—like fixing up the entire yard so beautifully—the value has increased a lot. More than a lot. Edna says it's up to $120,000! I got in touch with the landlord, and he's knocking down the price in recognition of all the work you put in. With no commission for seller or buyer, I've got more than I need to close the deal. I had over $15,000 saved before we left Minnesota, and with your rent checks, Bruno—I've saved every one of them—let's just say I have a substantial down payment. The landlord wants to carry a contract for deed on the balance, and Edna and I figured my monthly costs with taxes and insurance will be $100 less than I pay now. I'm jumping out of my skin with excitement!"

When Betty finally stopped speaking, I stood up and pulled her out of her chair and swung her in circles around the room. When I set her down, Anthony gave her a long hug before we all three tumbled back into our chairs. "It's the start of your happy ending, Betty," I said. "You deserve it."

Her closing was set for July 10, which gave us plenty of time to arrange a fantastic house warming party. For our gift to Betty, we installed a state-of-the-art barbecue in her back yard. "An ironic gift for the girl who hates parties," she said. "But also a perfect one. If I'm going to own the place, I want to be neighborly."

Neighborly was an understatement for the extravaganza we pulled off. Nearly a hundred guests circulated through Betty's backyard. To her delight, Ricardo made an appearance, and of course Rosa brought Luigi and the girls. As I ducked into the kitchen to get more ice for the cooler, I saw a familiar silhouette backlit by the low, horizontal rays of the late afternoon sun. No, I thought, it can't be. But it was.

My father's appearance was a complete shock to us all. He had arranged to make a surprise visit from Brasilia, Rosa told me, just for this occasion. I was beyond touched by his show of support for Betty, but more pressingly, I had no idea how to introduce him to Anthony. I didn't like the idea of lying, not even by omission.

At the same time, I still remembered too clearly the twist of my father's lips when he told me thinking of two men together "in that way" made him sick. Especially considering his fraught relationship with his own father, was it even fair to ask Anthony to meet mine? Ricardo's reaction had defied my highest, undreamed of hopes. Surely introducing Anthony now to my father was asking for trouble.

To buy time, I busied myself. I whacked away at the ice with a hammer until the unwieldy mass of soldered-together cubes became a bag of fine shards. I greeted each new arrival personally and at length. I insisted on manning the grill myself. A firm hand wrapped around my wrist and took the long-handled spatula from me. "Bruno," Anthony said, "stop hiding."

"I'm grilling, not hiding," I replied.

"You know I understand more than anyone here why your father's visit is not simply a happy surprise."

"It's not simply anything."

"I know."

"You didn't—he—did you speak to each other?"

"No, no. I'm just part of the crowd to him. Whatever you want to do, I'll be fine. Introduce us, don't introduce us, I'll be OK. I can be whoever you need me to be today."

"I'm not ashamed of you, of us."

"Us is another thing that will never be simple, not in this lifetime."

Just then, as if to underline his point, Betty appeared.

"Bruno, your father is looking for you," she hissed. "I mean, obviously, he can see you. But he asked me where you are and, well, I think he doesn't know how to come over and say hello to you himself, and I'm the last person . . . ."

"It's OK, Betty," I said. Suddenly overcome, I wrapped her in my arms and kissed both of her cheeks in succession.

"Ugh, you're sweaty!" she said, pushing me away.

"I'm burnin' up, burnin' up for your love," I sang, throwing my best Madonna pout her way. I felt suddenly carefree. My life wasn't simple, but it was good. Before my confidence faltered, I made my way over to my father.

He spoke first. "You did all this?" He tilted his head to indicate the festive spread.

"I did, yes, but not alone. My—Anthony," I pointed to where he stood, manning my post at the grill. "I couldn't have done it without him. He and I, we, we live together, Dad."

My father cleared his throat explosively. "*Meu filho*, I was wrong, what I said before. I see now that you never took advantage of Betty, not in the slightest. As far as your, well, your other relationships, I've never seen you so at peace. You look happy, Bruno."

"I am."

"And that has something to do with this Anthony, I take it?"

"More than I can say."

"Well." He cleared his throat again, more calmly this time. "I think I should shake his hand."

We walked back to the grill together, his long strides carrying him ahead of me as always. He stopped about a foot from Anthony and waited, hands laced together.

"Anthony, I'd like you to meet someone," I said. "This is my father, Rudolfo. Dad, this is Anthony, the man I live with."

My father extended his hand. Anthony met it, and they shook once.

"I'm pleased to make your acquaintance," my father said formally. Then, "Well. Time for a cigarette."

When the last of the guests had straggled home, the yard strewn with paper plates and empty beer bottles, I asked my father about my mother. "She's far too ill to travel," he said, "and far too confused to know where I am or, at times, even who I am. You have nothing to hide from her now, Bruno." His cheeks looked so gaunt in the glare of the streetlamp. When had everything changed? My beautiful, beautiful mother. I would have to return to Brasilia with him to say goodbye before it was too late.

Chapter Twelve

Song for My Mother

After two weeks in Miami, my father was tired, anxious, and more than ready to go back home. He looked so much older than I remembered him. It made me scared for not just him, but also my mother. I, too, was anxious to get to Brasilia as soon as possible. Once the logistics were finalized, the weight and reality of the trip smacked into me like a runaway train. I had been away from home for more than three years.

Rosa and Ricardo drove us to the airport. They sent their love to Mother but neither of them felt a need to see her. They had said their final good-byes when she was here. She was failing then and they wanted to remember her as she was. I was always "Mama's boy" and I needed to see her and be with her one more time.

When we finally arrived in beautiful Brasilia, the thrill of re-encountering my native city's sights and smells and sounds vanished almost immediately. The hardest moments with my mother came when her eyes were open. She didn't look at me, she looked through me, agitated and confused, demanding to know who I was. She fluttered in and out of consciousness, sleeping most of the time. Her clearest thoughts were of the past: her parents, her girlhood, the early days of her marriage to my father.

I brought a tape recording of my mother's favorite song with me, and a small cassette player. Over and over I played it, "Song for My Mother," an especially gorgeous Manfredo Fest song, performed by him and written by his wife Lili. It was her favorite. When it was playing she seemed calmer, as if the familiar tune helped to settle her restless mind.

I arranged to stay in Brasilia for an extra two weeks. During the middle of the third week of my stay, my mother died in her sleep while I sat on a chair beside her bed. I wrote to Anthony the night she passed away. "I'm so grateful I saw her," I told him. "I can't help but wonder if my being here helped her make the transition to wherever it is that she has gone. I feel as if maybe she was ready to die, and my saying goodbye gave her the last permission she needed. If so, I'm glad, because it was shocking for me to see how her quality of life had crumbled. She wasn't even herself in the true sense of the word; she wasn't the woman I have always known as my mother. It still hurts that she never knew who I really am. That she never met you. But if that ignorance gave her even a scrap more peace, then the sacrifice is nothing to me. My father may have been more right than I knew."

My mother was buried on a Thursday. I felt thankful to be by my father's side at the funeral as he greeted the throngs of friends and government dignitaries. To their deep dismay, none of my siblings, not even my globe-trotting brother, had been able to make it to Brasilia in time to attend. Though their absence was felt, the outpouring of emotion from those who were there was extraordinary. My mother had been dearly loved by all who knew her. Facing the grief of so many made it more possible, somehow, to acknowledge my own.

I landed in Miami just as the glitter of the winter holidays went up, bringing with it a full crop of party invitations. Although it all felt a little grotesque in light of my mother's death, the distraction helped push me through the confused aftermath—at least temporarily. When the Christmas tree came down, and the doldrums of late January arrived in earnest, I circled back to a dream begun on that trip to Brasilia. I wanted to show the country I loved so much to the man I loved so much. As winter wore on, I talked more and more to Anthony about Brasilia and about Itajai, where most of my extended family still lived, and about Santa Catarina and its beautiful beaches, especially Armacao, where much of my family spent the summer months.

Not only did I have a dream, I had a full-blown plan and the will to make it happen. Since I no longer had to pay a portion of Betty's rent, I began saving part of every paycheck—and those checks were sizeable. I was the most popular aerobics teacher at the center; all my classes had waiting lists. My goal was to save enough for a long trip to Brazil with Anthony, an indefinite sojourn. Why not experience life together in an entirely new way, outside of the intensity of Miami and the familiar rhythms of what had become our daily routine? "We're still young," I told him. "And we won't always be." As the weeks and months passed we talked more and more about the trip until, by the time we bought our tickets to Rio de Janeiro in August, it seemed we could barely think of anything else, let alone talk about anything else.

Once our departure date was set, I called Ricardo to tell him about the trip and to get a better sense of his own travel plans for the time we would be in Brazil. "Why don't you come over to the house tomorrow so we can talk about all this in person?" Ricardo said. "Bring Anthony with you. I have some ideas I'd like to explore with both of you."

The caretaker was waiting at the gate when we arrived. He led us directly to Ricardo, who was swimming laps in the pool. After he toweled off, he cut straight to the chase. "I wish I could go along with you to Brazil, but unfortunately I have business dealings here that require my attention. I need to send something with you, however. And I need you to keep everything I am about to tell you strictly confidential. Of course you have the right to refuse my proposal— that goes without saying. But I doubt you will. The request is very simple. I give you two large suitcases for you to use for your trip. In the lining of each of these two suitcases will be $200,000 worth of one hundred dollar bills, for a total of $400,000. Half of the money you deposit in Rio, and the other half in Florianopolis. If you agree, there's a generous payoff in it for you. Now it is up to you if you want to hear more."

Anthony's eyes were huge and he had started to rise from his chair. I grabbed his hand and held it firmly as he stood warily behind me. "Surely we'll be taking a risk in carrying so much cash in suitcases across international borders," I said. Anthony sat back down cautiously, perched on the edge of his lounge chair as if it was wet or dirty, though of course it was neither. The reflection of the noontime sun was brilliant against the smooth surface of the water in Ricardo's pool, so much so that I had to shield my eyes.

"No, I assure you, you would be in no danger," my brother

said calmly. "Passing through security here in the U.S., it will be impossible to detect the bills in the suitcases. On the other side, I have an associate who is a customs agent in Brazil. He will see to it that your luggage is not checked. As I mentioned, you will be compensated generously. When the money is deposited, I will give you 5 percent, or $20,000—half when you deposit it in Rio, at a special location of the Banco do Brazil. You keep your amount and deposit only $190,000. And the other half when you do the same upon arrival in Florianopolis."

Neither Anthony nor I said a word.

"Well," Ricardo laughed and took a sip of his scotch. "It looks like I've finally left you speechless—no easy feat. Come now, share your thoughts on my proposition."

"I trust you Ricardo," I said finally. "And the compensation you're offering, I've never had that amount of money in my life. It's beyond imagining. It will certainly give us a good time in Brazil."

Ricardo chuckled appreciatively. "When do you leave?" he asked.

"September 2, the 10 p.m. flight on Delta."

"I'll have the suitcases delivered to your apartment on the first."

As soon as we were passed through Ricardo's gate, Anthony and I stopped and stared at each other. The scent of jasmine hung heavily in the air, and the humidity was so thick that a bead of sweat trickled down from Anthony's hairline though he was standing stock-still. I could tell from the tension in the muscles at the corners of his jaw that he was angry. I was the one to eventually break the silence. "I've had suspicions over the years," I said, "that my brother is not exporting oranges from Brazil to the Azores on his mighty yacht, but maybe a white powder instead. But I'll never ask."

"I don't like it," Anthony snapped. "It's immoral. Not asking is one thing. Helping is another."

"We have no knowledge of exactly what we're helping with," I said. "I don't need to know and neither do you. What I do know is that this kind of money will give us a real start in Brazil. Anthony, this is for us, for what we're building together! We won't have another break like this one."

Anthony looked away, staring out his passenger window as I drove back toward Kendall. Finally, he turned back to me and said, "This cannot, absolutely cannot, become some kind of regular way of life. I'll turn the other way once, but never again."

When I reached for his hand, he yanked it away, so I turned on the radio and drove without speaking.

CHAPTER THIRTEEN

Beginner's Luck

On the first day of September, two light brown Samsonite suitcases arrived at our condo, as promised. The suitcases were considerably scuffed and scratched, which surprised me. I had assumed they would be new, but on second thought, large sums of cash might travel better in well-worn ones.

Anthony had read that a stack of 28 hundred-dollar bills weighed one ounce, so this stash of $200,000, made up of 2,000 hundred-dollar bills, would weigh just over seven pounds. Maybe up to eight pounds, including the special lining. He insisted we keep that extra eight pounds per suitcase in mind while packing. I assured him our clothing was light, and we would easily be able to fit all we needed, even with the hidden weight. Besides, if we left something behind, we'd be able to pick it up in Rio. It would be fine. And I had promised Anthony that after we made the two deposits, we would never again get ourselves involved with my brother's "business dealings."

Betty drove us to the Miami airport the next day. "It's so hard to say goodbye without knowing when I'll see you again," she said when we reached the gate in the Delta section of the terminal. She actually blinked back tears and pulled a Kleenex from her purse.

"We'll be in touch, Betty, sooner than you think," I said. Anthony and I sandwiched her between us in a playful hug, then went about checking our luggage, and boarded the plane. I turned back before entering the boarding walk to give one last goodbye wave. Betty's expression wasn't happy, but I couldn't quite tell if it was more sadness or anger that cast the shadow. Either way, I felt a wave of gratitude rise up in my chest. If not for Betty, I wouldn't be an American citizen. I wouldn't know Anthony, I wouldn't have changed my lifestyle, maybe I wouldn't even be alive. Whatever came next, I pledged to myself, I would continue to live up to my commitment to Betty and to our marriage.

Anthony and I were seated side by side in the middle of the coach section of the plane. "I can't believe we're on our way," I said, grabbing Anthony's hand then dropping it quickly. I had no intention of attracting any unwanted attention, but the temptation to touch him was hard to resist. "Look, here we go, we're over the ocean!" He laughed to see me so exuberant. He, too, was excited, but not so much that he didn't fall straight to sleep as soon as we'd finished our dinner. Try as I might, I couldn't relax enough to follow suit. Eventually, I gave up and sat wide awake in the darkness of the plane, listening to the soft sounds of breathing all around me. I had yet to sleep when the lights came on in the cabin at 6 a.m. the next morning and the flight attendant announced that breakfast was on its way. Less than an hour later, we touched down on the runway in Rio.

I started talking nonstop the moment we stepped off the plane. The colors, the smells, and maybe most of all the sounds of Portuguese all around me had me delirious. The lack of sleep could have been a factor, too. I chatted with everyone in earshot as we waited in the line for immigration inspection, stopping only long enough to follow the rules and show my passport when Anthony and I reached the checkpoint. Next, we retrieved our suitcases from baggage claim and went directly to the right side of the customs lines. Finally, my urge to talk fell away. The suitcases. I did recognize the agent from the photograph my brother had given me, just as he had promised I would. I casually introduced myself in Portuguese, saying, "My friend and I are eager to get going. I'll be showing Anthony around Rio." The customs agent smiled and waved us along without opening a single piece of our baggage.

Out in the heat of the morning, the airport road was choked with cabs. I held out my arm and seconds later one was at the curb, door open. I gave the driver directions. We'd be staying first with my friend Paulo, his wife Dina, and their two-year-old daughter. I knew Paulo from my boyhood days in Florianopolis. The way the United States had called to me, Rio had called to Paulo. He met Dina there, and since their engagement six years ago, he'd barely stepped outside the city limits. "They live between Ipanema Beach and Copacabana Beach on the Morro do Pavao," I reminded Anthony. "It's a small *favela* called Pavaozinho." I went on to explain, as I had a multitude of times before, that although a favela was considered a kind of slum, I had been to Paulo's before I left Brazil and it was perfectly pleasant.

I pointed out the open window of the cab, narrating to Anthony as we crawled through the endless traffic. Most of Rio's favelas were built high up on the hills. "They have spectacular panoramic views of the ocean," I said. "Of course, those who can afford it live below, nearer to the water. But one in five Cariocas—that's what we call people who live in Rio—lives in a favela. Some are nicer than others, some are just wastelands, hell on earth, unspeakably dangerous. In recent years drug lords have taken over some of the neighborhoods, and even the police are afraid to go there. But you don't need to worry. Pavaozinho isn't known for violence or drug trafficking. It may not be up to your princely standards, but then again, not much is . . . . Anyway, if you can suppress your snobby upbringing, I think you'll see the charm of their house. He and Dina and their daughter Gabriela live on the second floor—they've got a living room, a kitchen, and two bedrooms—and Dina's parents live on the first floor."

Brazilian tradition held that whenever adult children married, their parents would just add a story to the house, with the stairway on the outside. So this kind of arrangement was incredibly common. "You'll often see four stories and even more," I told Anthony, "depending on how many children are in a family. It's just Paulo and Dina and Gabriela above her parents, though. You'll like them. They're our age and they're a riot to be around."

The taxi ride was in and of itself an exhilarating tour of Rio's highlights. We wended our way past Copacabana, then to Ipanema, and then we took Rua Teixeira de Melo to the Morro do Pavao. There the taxi came to a dead stop. It was 9 a.m., rush hour's peak, and we were trapped in thick, immovable traffic. Finally the driver pulled up to the corner of an especially narrow street and said, "Este é o mais proximo que eu vou chegar. This is the closest I'll get."

Slightly confused, we grabbed the two Samsonite suitcases, paid our fare, and started walking up the street toward Paulo's. He must have heard us coming, because he opened the door the minute I knocked. "Bruno, you made good time!" he said. "I've been waiting for you so I can put you right to work. Hah! But seriously, we have to leave. I'll explain later. For now, Dina will take good care of your things. Let's go, we need to hurry."

After the most abbreviated introductions between Anthony and a very pregnant Dina, Paulo herded us to his VW bus. We'd barely closed the van doors when he tore away from the curb. "Paulo, old friend," I laughed, "What's the mad rush? Where are you taking us?" I asked.

"To the beach," he said, "to work. Your timing with this visit is perfect. I need you here. Dina can't lift anything and shouldn't leave the house—you can see she'll be having that baby any minute now. I've been trying to keep our business going solo, and her parents have been great about helping us with Gabriela, but I could really use your help, man. You'll see what I mean."

Ten minutes later, we were at Ipanema Beach. Clear blue water and white sand stretched for what looked like miles under the high morning sun. Paulo stopped the van right in front of Posto 9, then instructed us to start unloading. Despite not sleeping at all on the plane, or maybe because of it, I was practically manic. I set to unpacking the bus in record speed while Anthony struggled to keep up. Between the three of us, the entire van was empty in five minutes. "Now, stay right here," Paulo said. "I have to park the bus, then I'll be right back to show you what to do."

When he reappeared, he finally slowed down enough to explain what was actually going on. "This, what you see here"—he raised his palm toward a pile of six aluminum poles and a roll of canvas on the ground—is the business that Dina and I run, right on Ipanema Beach. We set up this tent, and from there, the money rolls in just like the ocean waves." He laughed. "Throngs of Brazilians and foreigners come here to enjoy this beautiful beach, and we fulfill their every need—beach chairs, sun umbrellas, piles of refreshments." He pointed to the three enormous coolers next to the poles and canvas. "We've got Coca Cola, Fanta, beer—Antarctica or Itaipava—bottled water, and the most popular of all, caipirinha." Caipirinha was made of fresh lime juice, sugar, and ice mixed with either gin or cachaca, a liquor made from sugar cane. Once we lugged the three huge coolers filled with these refreshments to the tent, Paulo hung his vendor sign, which identified this particular structure as Barraca do Paulo – 121, or "Paul's Shack Number 121."

We worked the beach until 5 p.m. that evening, then packed everything up, loaded it back into the VW bus, and headed back to Paulo's where Dina had dinner waiting. The smell alone had me practically drooling: *feijoada* made just right with smoky *choriço* sausage, salty *carne seca*, and, Dina proudly assured us, not only beef ribs, but tongue as well. As is traditional, she served the stew with kale sautéed in olive oil with onions and garlic, white rice, an orange slice, and a sprinkle of *farofa* (toasted cassava flour).

When we had gorged ourselves, Dina began to clear the dishes from the wooden kitchen table, but Paulo waved to her to sit back down. "I have to tell you the news," he said. "And you need to be sitting, Dina, because you're not going to believe it. I counted the money we earned at the barraca today—it was double the normal amount for this time of the year. Double! Now, I know you were both running all over the place, but that doesn't explain these sales. How did you do it?"

"Beginner's luck?" I said.

But it was not beginner's luck, which I knew even as I pretended it was. The next day was even more wildly successful than the first. The fact was, my personality was ideally suited to the life of a beach vendor. I had the perfect touch with customers, a sharp instinct for the business, and enormous ambition. Like when a customer asked for a sandwich, for example. Paulo and Dina didn't actually stock sandwiches at their barraca, but did that stop me? No, it did not. Not even close. I ran—sprinted, in fact—two blocks down the beach to get the sandwiches made at another barraca, then brought them back and charged the tourists double what I paid. And that's the thing: vacationers don't mind paying double the price to avoid the hassle of walking there themselves.

It helped that Paulo had scored the ideal spot for his barraca. The beaches of Rio are divided into sections called postos, each with its own lifeguard and bathroom facilities. Ipanema stretches from Posto 7 through 10, and Posto 9, where Paulo set up his barrack, was the most popular of all. Part of the draw to Posto 9 was the "tall and tan and young and lovely girl from Ipanema," a mythical creature made famous by a song written by Antonio Carlos Jobim and Vinicius de Morais in the early 1960s. The duo had reportedly written the song as they sat in a bar watching a beautiful young girl who drifted by on her way to the beach. Local legend held that the girl from Ipanema still came regularly to bathe right at the end of Posto 9, called Rua Vinicius de Morais. The story captivated locals and tourists alike. Paulo was damn lucky to get such a prime location.

On our third day in Rio, I decided the time had come to deal with the Samsonite suitcases—or more specifically, with their secret cargo. I explained to Paulo over breakfast that I had some business to do. "But don't worry. Anthony will go with you, and I'll grab a taxi and join you just as soon as I'm finished."

Anthony cast me a look saying, "I don't like manning the barraca without you," and "I don't like what you're going to do," all without opening his mouth. He might not like it, but I had to take care of business. Certainly he wasn't going to! And it was too late to back out.

Once Paulo and Anthony headed out and Dina was busy at the kitchen sink washing the breakfast dishes with "help," it was time to dismantle the suitcase. I tore out the lining and there, as promised, was the cash—all $200,000. Slowly and carefully, I counted and then recounted 5 percent of the bills, or $10,000. That was our portion. I placed those bills carefully in the pockets of the suitcase and locked it. Then I loaded the rest of the bills into a zipped pouch inside my backpack and walked out the door.

Getting from the favela to the bank was substantially more difficult than I had anticipated. The only artery into the favela was a narrow cobblestone path—not even an alley, really—and between that and the ungodly traffic congestion, the only vehicles that could get in were motorcycle taxis. Now it all made sense, how our driver had left Anthony and me off at the favela's edge when we first arrived. There was simply no way he could have gotten us any closer. I hailed a passing bike and explained to the driver that I was headed to a specific bank on Rua Barrata Ribeiro in Copacabana. He knew the bank well. "*E muito perto, so tres kilometros daqui,*" he said. "It's close, only three kilometers."

After I negotiated the fare, I climbed on the back and grabbed hold of the driver, delighted for what was to come. We snaked along at least twice as fast as the speed of traffic, riding between lanes and shaving dangerously close to every car we passed. Quickly, almost too quickly, we arrived at the bank. After the driver took my *reais* and shot back off into traffic, I adjusted the straps of the backpack, took a deep breath, and walked inside. Directly past the doors stood a uniformed attendant. I asked him to direct me to the bank manager Ricardo had named. "Straight ahead and to your left," he said, pointing to a thin man of about fifty, hair slicked back severely, with a narrow, downturned mouth and thin, metal-framed reading glasses.

He was seated at the second desk in a row of three. I sat down on one of the chairs across the desk from him and watched as he counted the bills rapidly, then provided a deposit slip for me to sign on behalf of Ricardo. Easy as that. I stood up and walked right back out through the sparkling glass doors. It was all so casual, so effortless, right down to the cab that was immediately available to take me to Ipanema Beach, Posto 9.

When I finally arrived at Paulo's barraca, Anthony was beside himself. "It's about time you got here!" He was running his fingers through his hair. "Everyone is going crazy: 'Where's Bruno? When will Bruno be back?' They're driving me insane." I knew his anxiety had more to do with my errand than the barraca customers. But with Paulo right there, I couldn't exactly bring Anthony up to speed on the events of my morning.

"Well I'm here now, and it's all alright! Feel free to announce it to the masses," I said, hoping he could tell from my tone that the bank run had gone off without a hitch.

That evening, Paulo finally spoke what I could tell had been on his mind since our first day on the beach. "I don't know when you plan to leave Rio," he said, "and the thing is, I can't afford for you to go! Please stay at least until the baby is born and Dina can return to work." His face was earnest. "I'm not asking you to volunteer. I'll pay you generously, in fact, I'll pay you half of all our profits and not a penny less. That's half of every dollar we take in after expenses. I'll show you the books if you want. And you can stay here, of course—although you may not want to continue sleeping on esteiras on the floor."

"I've been sleeping fine," I said. In all honestly, the *esteiras*, straw mattresses, were pretty torturous.

"How about you, Anthony?" Paulo's face looked so hopeful.

"It takes a little getting used to," Anthony said, never one to dance around the truth. "But I'm surviving."

"Listen," Paulo said. "I understand if you want to get on with your trip. If you did decide to stay, I'd be in your debt, even with the split profits. No hard feelings, no matter what you do. The point I really want to make here is that I know you're—well, whatever the two of you are to each other, and you're fine. You're fine by me. Fine by Dina. You're family here, both of you, just as you are. I need to say that out loud, I need you to know where I stand on this. Am I clear?" He stood and placed one hand on my shoulder and one on Anthony's. "You guys, you're my angels," he said. "Sent straight from God, and I mean that." He turned and walked out.

Anthony and I sat there at the dining table in silence, staring at each other in the dim glow of the overhead light. Finally Anthony broke the silence. "You," he whispered, "have a knack for surrounding yourself with the kind of people I didn't know really existed in this mean, miserable world. People with hearts, Bruno. Good hearts. Hearts like yours."

Later that very same night—it was September 5—Anthony and I woke to moaning through the bedroom wall. "Dina must be in labor," I said. "Roll over and go back to sleep." Anthony dutifully rolled over and we both tried our best to sleep through the commotion, but that idea proved to be a pipe dream. All night we could hear the low murmur of happy conversation punctuated by sharp exclamations marking Dina's contractions. The unfamiliar voice in the mix—reassuring but firm—had to be the midwife, we guessed. The sun had just risen high enough to cast a thin, gray light through our window when we heard a shaky wail, and then Paulo's excited shouts: "It's a boy! A son!" The midwife, when she emerged, told us the new baby weighed a healthy three and a half kilograms, or a little over seven pounds.

Paulo and Dina named the baby Bruninho, after me. "You're so good, Bruno," Anthony said to me later as we settled down to nap, exhausted from the long, wakeful night and the excitement of the morning. "Not just good to me, but to everyone in your orbit. I'll stay, if you want to. I know you do. Your face gives it all away."

We committed to stay for another six weeks, when Dina would be able to safely return to work again. The next day, I volunteered to make dinner—an outrageous seafood feast for everyone, including Dina's parents. I found everything I needed at the nearby market, and Anthony surprised us all with a bottle of fine French Champagne to toast the baby's arrival. "To a bright future filled with health and prosperity!" Paulo boomed.

I enjoyed our work at the beautiful beach more and more as the weeks passed. Even Anthony seemed to be genuinely enjoying himself. "You know," I said one day, "Santa Catarina has a dozen beaches like this—even more beautiful, in fact—and we'll be getting there before Christmas, which is the start of the busiest vacation time in Southern Brazil. What I'm getting at is, what if we set up this kind of business there, at one of the popular beaches?"

"It's a lot of fun, I admit," Anthony said. "My father would go apoplectic over the idea of me as a beach vendor, and I doubt the rest of my family, or even my friends from the old days, would react much better. But the thing is, when I ignore that snooty voice in my head, as you're always encouraging me to, I like doing this. I like meeting people and being out in the fresh air. And I make a mean caipirinha now. Plus, I enjoy watching you work the crowds. Not to mention, if the beaches on Santa Catarina are anywhere near this busy, we could rake in the cash."

By the fifth week, Dina was anxious to get back to work and her mother was anxious to have Gabriela returned to her care, and to take charge of baby Bruninho as well. "This is it, my friends," I announced at dinner one night. "The big day is drawing near. Time for you to get back to your normal life without two extra men in the house! Anthony and I will be leaving early next week."

"I can't find the words to thank you for your help these past weeks," Paulo said. "There's no way I could have gotten through this without you guys."

"Angels," Dina said. "Paulo is right. You two were sent by God. We only want to know that you'll visit again! And you have to tell us where you'll go next so we can write and call."

"To Brasilia," I said. "I want to show Anthony the city my father helped to build. October is coming to an end, and we want to see him there before he takes off for Santa Catarina and his summer home."

"Wonderful!" Paulo said, "but please do come back soon and stay with us. If you do, I promise not to work you so hard."

The following Wednesday, Anthony and I left for Brasilia on the Brazilian airline, Varig. When we landed, my father was waiting for us at the airport. He hugged me long and hard, and I was surprised to see that his eyes were red. He had been crying! Each time I saw him, since that night in Anna's and Jim's sunroom, the depth of his love for me was becoming clearer. This was enough of a surprise, but when he also embraced Anthony, I knew that despite his struggle with my homosexuality, he would never let it come between us. As much as I was grateful for that, I also ached for Anthony. To imagine my own father turning a cold, hard back to me as Anthony's father had done—that's the kind of wound that can fester forever.

Chapter Fourteen

Ventures

By the third week of November we left Brasilia to make our way to Florianopolis, and then on to Santa Catarina. My father agreed to meet us at his home in Armacao the following week. Our flight from Rio to Florianopolis had just one stop: Curitiba, the capital city of the state of Parana. From Curitiba, a commuter flight could take us easily to the city of Foz do Iguaçu, which in and of itself was nothing spectacular except that it was situated just twenty kilometers from one of the most breathtaking sights in the world, Iguaçu Falls. My parents had taken Rosa, Ricardo, and me to visit those roaring waters almost every summer of our childhood. My mother had been especially partial to the falls. I couldn't pass up the opportunity to share one of my favorite places in the world with Anthony.

So we stayed overnight. The next morning, as we waited in line for the first bus to the falls, Anthony said,"I have to admit, I was in a hurry to get to Florianopolis. But now that we're here, I can't wait to see this so-called wonder of the world."

"It's so-called for good reason," I said. "And you know what? I've never brought someone to see the falls before. You'll be my first."

"I didn't know you had any firsts left," he said in mock astonishment.

"Shh, don't spoil the moment."

Once off the bus, the roar of water against rock was thunderous. We slipped into the fast flowing throng of tourists from all over the world and headed out on the walkway. I barely looked at the water; instead, I watched Anthony's face. It is impossible to describe the experience of seeing Iguaçu for the first time. It's not a single waterfall, but rather a contiguous chain of falling water that spans almost two miles and towers between two hundred and three hundred feet from top to bottom. The concrete and steel walkways extend into the river basin, right into the rapids. "Look as far as you can that way," I said, pointing behind us to the north. "That's Paraguay. The falls are visible there, too. You can see this water from three separate countries."

Mists from the falls drifted across the walkways. We stood at the platform railing, silent, soaking it in.

"Let's do that!" Anthony said, pointing to a boat on the wide river, taking tourists right up to the base of the falls.

"We'll get wet, you realize?"

"Bruno, this is a once in a lifetime moment! I don't want to be foolhardy, but the results from those viral load tests we took right before we left were excellent. I think we can handle getting a little damp."

I laughed. "You? Foolhardy? Never. We'll get more drenched than damp, but I'm up for it if you are."

I imagined then and there what it would be like to kiss

Anthony on the boat under the falls. I mean, really kiss him, on the mouth. But of course, that would never be possible in a public setting like this.

The next morning we took one last look at Iguaçu before catching our connection back to Curitiba, and from there, finally, Florianopolis. I couldn't wait to finally share the island paradise of my childhood with Anthony, and I was thrilled that the sun was still above the horizon as we began our descent. From the plane we had a bird's eye view of all forty-two of Santa Catarina's sugar sand beaches. Anthony was utterly enchanted. "As soon as we land I need to find a phone so I can call Matilda," I said as he stared wide-eyed out the small plane window.

"Matilda—cousin on your dad's side of the family, right?"

"God, you've got a memory that doesn't quit! Yes, she's the daughter of my dad's brother, Luiz. He and his family have a summer home near ours." Our plane touched down with a lurch and, screeching, came to a halt on the tiny landing strip. We climbed down the plane's stairs and made our way across the tarmac to the cinderblock airport to find a pay phone.

Matilda answered on the first ring. "Bruno! I can't believe you're finally here!" She squealed so loudly into the phone that I held it away from my ear, winking at Anthony. "I'll get in the car right now and be at the airport to pick you up in a half hour or less!" she promised. "Don't move a muscle!"

"Not even to sit down and rest my weary legs?" I teased her.

"Oh, you," she said. "I'm hanging up now! I'll see you soon, *meu primo!*"

Anthony and I walked to a small grassy area with two wooden benches and a drinking fountain. Everything here in

Florianopolis—even the plain, ordinary things like the landing strip, the drinking fountain, the cinderblock walls of the airport— looked beautiful to me. It had been four years since I'd been back to the island, and I had not realized how terribly I missed it. Suddenly I wondered if Matilda would know me when she saw me, and if I would know her.

But I needn't have worried. Matilda knew me as soon as she pulled up in her VW Combi. She threw her arms first around me, and then Anthony. Finally, after the hugs and the kisses and the introduction, we were on the road.

My grandfather wasn't the only one of his siblings who'd had the good sense and good fortune to purchase land near Armacao Beach. Most of his brothers and sisters had done the same, and now their children's families and even their grandchildren's families were expanding and building homes of their own as well. Armacao was my ancestral home turf, a village filled with family members in nearly every house and cottage.

The first thing we had to do when we arrived was to go knock on doors up and down the street to greet the many aunts, uncles, and cousins I had there. Everyone welcomed Anthony warmly enough, though I sensed that questions about my male companion lurked just below their smiles. Anthony, by now, had excellent command of Portuguese, but his accent gave him away as a native Spanish speaker. He explained, time after time, that though we met in Miami, he was born in Venezuela. My relatives exclaimed that his Spanish would come in handy, reminding me that the island was a favorite vacation spot for Argentines since the border was easily within driving distance.

The next day I borrowed the car my father always left on his property to take Anthony on a tour of Santa Catarina. Dad bought American whenever possible, so his car in Armacao was a three-year-old Chevy Impala. "Not a bad ride, considering," I said as I navigated the bumpy gravel roads to Florianopolis. We'd gotten an early start, heading straight to Florianopolis to deposit Ricardo's money in the Banco do Brasil, exactly as he had specified.

"I'll wait in the car," Anthony said when we pulled up to the bank. He buried his head in his arms and mumbled, "See no evil, hear no evil . . . just hurry up and get it over with."

"You're going to have to come in if you want your name on the account," I pointed out. Reluctantly, he followed me in to the tiny island bank. The whole process—depositing the remaining $190,000 in Ricardo's name, then opening a new account and depositing the $20,000 we had received as compensation—was carried out slickly.

"What a relief," Anthony said as we left. "I feel like I can take a deep breath for the first time since we got here. No more worrying about getting robbed."

"And we can finally launch our business," I said.

For the rest of the day we circled the island, taking in all its splendor. We ate dinner at a restaurant in the center of Florianopolis, right next to the lovely central square. It was 9 p.m., the height of Brazil's dinner hour, so the restaurant was full, couples at every table. As we ate, Anthony threw me question after question. "It thrills me," I told him,"to see you so excited about this place that I love so much. I think I love you even more than I already did . . . ."

Anthony slipped his hand discreetly beneath the table, and traced my kneecap with his thumb. "I feel exactly the same," he said. "This might sound premature, I mean, it's only been a day, but I can see a future for us here. What is it about you that makes me feel so sure I'm moving in the right direction?"

It was a clear night, and the stars in the night sky shone with an unusual brightness. Maybe it was just being on the island, away from the big city lights, or maybe it was some kind of celestial phenomenon. Either way, it was breathtaking. Anthony and I strolled through the square, talking over our plan. "There's no reason for us to rush into anything as far as housing," I said. "We don't need to decide until my father arrives from Brasilia next week, at the earliest."

On the drive back to Armacao, the exhaustion from our nonstop day of touring, and the long day of traveling before that, caught up to us. "Tomorrow," I said,"we're sleeping in until we feel like getting up. And then, once we've taken our sweet ass time having breakfast—I'll cook for you, a delicious Brazilian breakfast feast, just you wait—then we'll go to the beach and just lie there all day."

Apparently the weather approved of my plan, because we woke up to a perfectly clear sky and the kind of light breeze you need to enjoy the beach without overheating. As we basked in the sun, listening to the sound of the waves crashing in, one after the next, the most mesmerizing sound in the world, Anthony asked me what I was thinking about. "You look so dreamy," he said. "I have to know."

"Funny," I said, "because what I'm thinking about is cars. The perfect vehicle for our beach business would be a camioneta."

"Camioneta?"

"Paulo had one in Rio—that VW bus he hauled his stuff

around in. It's just a station wagon or a covered large van. They're hard to find but not impossible. We're just going to have to ask around."

On our way back from the beach, we stopped at every gas station in Florianopolis, announcing that we were trying to hunt down a used camioneta. When we got home, I called Matilda and asked her to put out the word, as well, and within forty-eight hours we had what we were looking for—a light gray VW bus just like Paulo's.

"It's a beauty!" I said. Anthony eyed the rust. "Nothing I can't fix easily," I said. "You didn't see what my VW bug looked like when I first bought it in Minnesota. But I worked my magic, and bam! Pristine. This one will be, too. Just wait, you'll see." All we had left to do was get the tent for our barraca and the goods we'd be selling out of it, and we'd be in business.

By the time my father arrived from Brasilia, I was so excited about our new business that I walked him through every detail all the way home from the airport. I don't think I stopped to take in a breath through the entire drive. In any case, Dad was convinced we were onto something and agreed to take us shopping the next day. He knew Florianopolis like the back of his hand, and with his help we quickly found the perfect aluminum poles for the barraca's frame and a cheery green and yellow striped canvas for the top. We bought beach chairs, beach towels, coolers, and refreshments, too, overstuffing Dad's car as well as our van.

Anthony watched me later as I measured and assembled the tent and hand painted our new sign with the words, *Barraca dos Estranjeiros*, The Foreigner's Shed. I could feel his eyes on me, and his obvious admiration excited me. I loved to impress him.

By the second week of December, we were finally ready. It was the beginning of the tourist season, which would gain steam all the way through February before starting its downward spiral. "But I want us to persevere until the end of May," I said to Anthony, "as long as the weather cooperates and the south winds blow in our favor."

On the second Saturday in December, we rose before dawn and drove our camioneta to the Praia de Joaquim to search for the perfect spot. We wanted to be where the best customers would be. It didn't take us long to scope out an area near the water and sand dunes—a great spot flat enough to set up our barraca and open up for business. We knocked it out of the park on the first day, and within a week we knew that not only had we picked a great spot, but also that the whole barraca business was a good move for us.

A last question to settle was housing. The drive from the beach back to my dad's would take at least half an hour, an exhausting prospect at the end of a long day in the sun. I was also convinced there was no need for us to do it. Surely, some family connection could lead to a place to stay in Lagoa. When I mentioned this to my father, he agreed.

"Simple. A cousin of mine has a summer house there. If for some reason you can't stay with him, I know he'll at least have other suggestions. I'll call him tomorrow."

The next day, he showed up at Joaquim Beach as we were folding it in for the day and said, "Come with me, and I'll show you your new place." We trailed his car in the camioneta to a beautiful gated home only three short blocks from Lagoa de Conceicao. My father parked, then opened the gate. As we drove onto the gracious property, Anthony said, "We could walk to work from here!"

"Only if you carry the tent, and the cooler," I replied.

Once we'd parked as well, we joined my father on the front lawn.

"This is the summer home of my cousin Nereu," he said. "Sadly, his wife Gloria has been very ill so they haven't been able to visit for a while. Anyway, he offered to turn the servants' quarters over to you. It's just over here, to the right of the driveway."

I'd seen how taken aback Anthony looked when my father used the phrase servants' quarters, but from what I knew of Nereu, I wasn't concerned. Sure enough, when my dad unlocked the door, we entered a full-fledged house with two spacious bedrooms, a bathroom with a tiled shower, a small living room with a TV and shelves lined with books, and a galley kitchen complete with a microwave.

"If this is where the help lives, all I can say is, wow," Anthony whispered to me.

"Nereu has visited so infrequently over the last few years, it hasn't made sense to have staff stay on," my father said. "He likes the idea of having someone living on the grounds, and insists that he won't allow you to pay any kind of rent. There's a security system installed on the property, but he's had break-ins twice, and says he worries all the time about burglaries and vandalism. It'll be a relief to him to know you're here."

He then handed me the keys, and a piece of paper with Nereu's number so I could contact him myself if need be.

With the housing question answered, we sank ourselves completely into the barraca. "I become this amplified version of myself in the crowd," I said one evening as we were loading the van. "I love chatting with people, making them smile and laugh and catering to their quirky needs. It's like a game for me, and the best part is when I win, I'm winning us money." Anthony went along with it all, getting into the swing of the barraca scene at his more cautious, methodical pace. He continued honing his talent for making killer caipirinhas and trading stories with tourists from all over the world.

CHAPTER FIFTEEN

Let Us Pray

Because we owned and operated our own business, we could take as many days off as we wished. Nonetheless we staked out our tent most days, unless there was foul weather. One thing I was firm about was not setting up the barraca if there was a strong south wind or heavy rain, which is just what happened on the third Sunday after we'd launched our business.

"Anthony," I said. "Let's go to mass instead."

Anthony looked sincerely stunned, an expression that he quickly exaggerated into mock shock and horror.

"Seriously, though," I said. "I know it's weird but I have my reasons. I'm not saying I want to rejoin the religious fold. But I do want to meet this priest—Padre Antonio. My cousin Matilda told me a friend of hers said his sermons are stellar. And I have something I want to ask him."

"And? Are you going to tell me what it is?"

"All things in time," I said. "Just trust me for a minute. Or try, anyway."

At exactly 10 a.m., we entered the double oak doors of the Lagoa da Conceicao Parish. The sermon did not live up to my cousin's praise. In fact, it was a little boring. I had forgotten how dry and distant liturgy could be. We were ready to leave right after communion, but first I wanted to find out where Padre Antonio lived. I scanned the aisles as we discreetly made our way to the rear of the church. A young mother sat in the last row, a sleeping a baby in her arms. "Excuse me," I said, "Can you tell me where the priest lives?" She pointed to a door set off to the side, and explained that behind it lay the entrance to the priest's adjoining apartment.

I thanked her, and we walked out of the sanctuary into the harsh sunlight. Anthony held in his questions until we arrived at our favorite lakeside restaurant, and set in on a leisurely lunch. "Now seems like a good time to fill me in on what's happening here," Anthony said.

"Church, you mean?"

"Bruno, come on. I've been a good sport, but I'd prefer to know why we're tracking down this priest before we show up at his door."

"I've heard things," I said. "About this priest and his congregation—his gay congregation. HIV and AIDS are a huge problem here, and he's struggling with those men. Matilda says he's even turned them away. We could help."

"We're not even members of the church. And we're gay and have HIV. Remember?"

"Exactly. We're gay and we have HIV, Anthony. And I don't know if you've noticed, but it's not exactly ruining our lives. But the guys here? I'm not saying I've got it all figured out. I don't. I'm just saying I want us to introduce ourselves."

He glanced down at his watch. "As long-winded as he was, the sermon should have wrapped up by now. Shall we?"

A housekeeper answered the door as soon as we knocked. "We're here to see Padre Antonio," I said.

"I'm sorry. It's almost time for his rest." She looked incredibly stern.

"It won't take long. We promise."

She disappeared into the apartment while Anthony and I waited outside the door. We looked at each other but said nothing, not with the door standing wide open like that. The housekeeper returned moments later and motioned us into the waiting room. "He'll see you," she said. "But remember, he's tired. He needs to rest soon."

Padre Antonio opened the waiting room door about ten minutes later. He looked irritated and even a little suspicious as he extended his left hand. "What can I do for you?"

I took his hand in mine and gripped it firmly. "My name is Bruno Garcia," I said. "I'm honored to meet you. This is my friend, Anthony Nunez. I'm originally from Itajai and spent my summers at Praia da Armacao. Anthony's from Venezuela, but we met in Miami in the United States."

The padre looked Anthony up and down. "Why do you call yourself Anthony? Isn't that the same as my name, Antonio?"

"My father insisted that I never let anyone call me Antonio or Tony," he explained, "but always Anthony. His roommate at the University of Michigan was named Anthony Bishop. He was one of my father's best friends. I was named after him. So, there you have it." Anthony laughed, but the padre said nothing. He just smiled a tight little smile.

"What can I do for you?" he asked again.

"We're here to offer our help," I said. "I'm going to come straight to the point, and trust you will keep this confidential. Anthony and I are both gay and we're both HIV positive. We know how things are here, the shunning, the disownment, the harassment. The danger of getting beat up, or worse. My guess is that many come to you for help. Am I right?"

Padre Antonio looked shocked. "Yes," he said, after a stretch of silence. "More and more are coming to me and I have nothing to offer them but prayer. Prayer is not enough. When it comes to practical support, I'm empty handed."

"Anthony and I would be willing to assist you there. Last week I went to the Florianopolis Health Department and asked about their ability to offer the drugs needed to control HIV. They told us they can get the drugs, but no one is asking for them." Anthony's eyebrows shot up. I hadn't told him about the trip to the health department. I wanted to get the groundwork underway before I did. I'm not sure why. Maybe to prove to him that I really was a new man, that I could help others the way he had helped me. "I have lived with the disease for years now," I continued, "as has Anthony—and as you can see, we're in good health. We're living normal and fulfilling lives. It's more possible than you would think, if you eat right, exercise, and take the recommended medication. We can share our knowledge and experience with your congregation, and others, whoever needs it. We can give them hope, but more importantly, we can give them a realistic means to fulfill that hope."

Padre Antonio began to cry softly. "Jesus has answered my prayers," he said.

"You are sent to me by the Virgin Mary whom I pray to every second of the day asking for help with this."

"This is how you can reach us," I said. I handed him a piece of paper on which I'd written out our home telephone number and address. "Any time. Whatever you need."

Padre Antonio kissed me on both of my cheeks, then kissed Anthony. "Thank you, thank you, thank you," he said. He followed us all the way to the front door, waving as we walked down the sidewalk to our van.

"I didn't expect him to be so grateful," I said after I shut the van door. "He really needs us."

Anthony said nothing. When I put my hand on his shoulder, thinking he was silent because he was weeping, he laughed out loud and then, at some point it wasn't just laughter anymore, it was also sobbing, laughing and sobbing at the same time. "I don't know what's come over me," he finally said. "But yes, Bruno, we have to help. We absolutely have to help."

Our visit with Padre Antonio was on December 28; I remember this because I was thinking that the timing of our meeting, so soon after Christmas, was either very good or very bad. The Christmas and New Year holidays come at the height of Brazil's vacation time, meaning our workdays at the barraca were longer and far more intense than ever until the vacation season tapered off.

As focused as I was on working as many hours as possible during the holiday, a mood struck me on the morning of December 31. As Anthony and I were loading the van for what would have been another twelve-hour day, I sidled up behind him and grabbed him around the waist. He yelled out in surprise and tried to wriggle free, but I had him in a tight grip made tighter yet when I hooked my thumbs into the belt loops of his blue jeans. "We need some time away from the barraca." I said. "I'm taking you to a New Year's Party!"

"You're crazy!" Anthony yanked away again, harder this time, and I unhooked my thumbs and loosened my hold so that he could spin around to face me. He glared at me, but I could see by the way he held the corners of his mouth in place that he was suppressing a smile despite his furrowed brow.

I took the full box of Styrofoam cups he'd been loading into the van, set it on the ground, and sat down on it. The box gave a little under my weight, and I stood back up. "Listen, Anthony, I just don't think you have any idea how the Brazilians celebrate New Year's Eve. No one does it like we do it."

"No one does anything quite like you do, Bruno. But you're the one who keeps saying we need to work longer hours on the beach, not shorter." He put his hands on his hips and set his jaw. "I can't defy the boss."

"Don't sass me," I teased. I smacked his ass playfully with a sleeve of Styrofoam cups. He glared at me again, but at the same time he looked obviously pleased. Anthony was nothing if not a flirt, and I loved to indulge him. Whenever we bantered this way, I felt like I was meeting him and falling in love for the first time. It happened again and again, this falling in love, and it made me feel like the luckiest man on earth. The curve of his mouth as he held back his grin, the seriousness of his dark eyes even as they glinted with mischief.

"As your boss," I said, thwacking the sleeve of cups against my palm, "I command you to come with me to the Grito de Carnaval."

The Grito de Carnaval, or the Carnival Yell marks the beginning of the Brazilian Carnival Season. In the United Stated Carnival is known as Mardi Gras (Fat Tuesday). In Brazil Carnival is the most important holiday of the year. This year it ends on February 20th. The following day is Ash Wednesday, which signals 40 days before Easter. We, Brazilians, actually start celebrating Carnival on New Years Eve. It is one of the best and craziest dance nights of the year because all of the new sambas are released. I couldn't wait to lose myself on the dance floor.

"Looks like you're going to get your way—as usual," Anthony said. "But it's not because you're my boss. It's because I can't resist you." He threw himself toward me, knocking me over easily and toppling us both over backward. He wrapped one arm behind my head protectively to cushion it as we landed on the gravel driveway. He tried to kiss me but we were both laughing too hard.

"I can't breathe," I coughed. "You maniac! Now get off me so we can load this van and get to the beach. The earlier we get to the beach, the earlier we leave. Let's go!"

We left Joaquin Beach around noon and headed for the family compound at Praia da Armacao. My father and his guests were dressed to the absolute hilt. Matilda had prepared an incredible meal of *paixada*, a seafood stew with lots of tomatoes, onions, garlic, fresh basil, and oregano, and two or three kinds of fresh fish cut in bite-size pieces. Then at the last minute, she heaped the shellfish into the simmering pot: shrimp, oysters, mussels, and clams.

We all sat at a long table in the garden of Matilda's house, visiting raucously and eating voraciously over the course of nearly three hours. When we were too full to even look at any more food, we finally headed to the beach. "This is where the real party begins," I told Anthony. "You won't believe the sight of the beach filled with fishermen and their families all dressed in white, like ghosts, or angels, hauling their little boats loaded with flowers for the *Rainha de Mar*, The Queen of the Sea. It's their offering in exchange for her blessings in the year ahead—Anthony, we should have brought flowers! What was I thinking? We need all the blessings we can get."

Just across the street from the beach was the New Year's Dance. The dance hall, an annex on the backside of the Catholic church, was swarming with brightly clothed people dancing in pairs and alone, exuding happiness. This was my opportunity to impress Anthony who had, oddly enough, never really seen me dance, other than a few steps here and there at neighborhood parties in Miami. I was not about to waste a chance to show him my talents. Obviously we couldn't dance together in such a public setting, but knowing his eyes were on me was the next best thing. I grabbed one cousin or friend after the next and glided through the throng of bodies. Everyone was enveloped in the music; we were a sea of dark heads swinging and shining under the lights. I felt transported, as if in a trance.

Anthony followed along with partners of his own, his eyes tracking every one of my steps as I moved faster and faster. He could barely keep up, and after a while he stopped trying. "Keep dancing, Bruno," he said as he stepped backward toward the cocktail table. "I want to watch you. I want to watch you like this forever." His face shone with sweat and happiness. So I danced on with the crowd of Brazilians while Anthony sipped his beer.

I was touching up the paint on our barraca sign on the first Tuesday morning after New Year's when Marta, Padre Antonio's housekeeper, came with a note. "It's urgent," she said.

"He wants you to come right away." I walked back into the house, where Anthony sat at the kitchen table with his coffee and the morning paper. Sun streamed in through the window behind him, forming what truly appeared to be a halo around his dark head.

"What now?" Anthony asked. He didn't look up. I had told him just a few minutes ago that we wouldn't be leaving for the beach for at least an hour since I was working on the sign.

"It's Padre Antonio. A young gay man named Alberto just got his HIV diagnosis."

Anthony stood up and swallowed the rest of his coffee in one fast gulp. "This is it, Bruno."

Marta met us at the entrance to the church and led us through the sanctuary, which was empty except for a few locals kneeling in prayer. When we reached the Padre's dark oak door, she paused and looked directly at me and then at Anthony. Finally, she stepped aside before she gently pulled it open. "Go ahead," she said. "He's ready."

Padre Antonio sat upright in his leather desk chair, which was swiveled out to face the bay window on the east wall. Across from him were three straight-backed wooden chairs. The two chairs closest to the door, where we stood motionless, were empty, but on the third chair nearest the window sat a young man of about twenty. He wore blue jeans and a long-sleeved, white cotton shirt. His elbows rested on his thighs and his face was buried in his hands. His shoulders—which I could see were broad and muscular, even through his shirt—rose and fell with the uneven ins and outs of his breath. Morning sun filtered through Padre's louvered blinds, casting stripes of light and shadow across the young man's back. Through the heavy closed door came the far-off sound of organ music. Apparently, the organist was practicing for the next Mass. Anthony caught my gaze and I knew he was thinking, as was I, that this was not going to be easy.

"Bruno, Anthony, this is Alberto," said Padre. "Alberto, these men are here to help. They know more about HIV and AIDS than I do. Much more."

"I know plenty about HIV," Alberto said into his hands. "I know about dying from it."

I sat down on the chair closest to Alberto and angled it toward him, and Anthony did the same, so that now our chairs formed a sort of tight triangle, with Padre just outside of it.

"Alberto," I said. "Who have you told about this?"

"No one! Just Padre. Do you think I'm an idiot?"

"What about your parents?" Anthony asked.

"I could never tell them. Never!" Alberto buried his face deeper into his hands and cried harder.

"I felt that way at first, too," I said. "When I was diagnosed with HIV, I was determined that I would never, ever tell my parents."

Alberto lifted his head a little. His eyes were shiny and red rimmed from crying and he looked as if he had not shaved for at least three days. Still, he brimmed over with the kind of beauty that belongs to the young alone.

"I don't know if I ever would have told my parents if it hadn't been for Anna and Jim," I said. "They are like my second parents, my American parents, and I was living with them in America at the time of my diagnosis. I love them like real family, and I trusted them. And they were convinced that I needed to talk to my father and tell him the truth."

"Did you do it?"

"Yes. And his reaction was nothing like I feared. Not that he fully understands my being gay, or how it is to live with HIV. I don't expect him to. But he loves me—I know that now beyond a shadow of a doubt. And he didn't turn me away. Not even close. In fact, he's the main reason Anthony and I are now in Florianopolis."

"And your mother?"

"No. I never told her. At my father's request, I promised I wouldn't." A lump rose in the back of my throat and I had to stop speaking. I felt a pressure beneath my clavicle. My mother's image rose within me so vividly that I could see the tiny lines around her eyes and smell the lilac soap that she used every day of her life. "Nothing is perfect," I said. "My mother was ill when I was diagnosed—losing her memory to the dementia that eventually killed her. My father said that the truth would break her heart and destroy her last remaining years of life. He asked for my word in keeping my sexuality and my disease a secret from her. I kept that promise until the day she died."

Padre Antonio listened intently.

"You might think Bruno sounds wise," said Anthony," and he is. But when I met him, he was such a wreck. He was throwing his life away—and he didn't even know it."

"Is that true?" Alberto looked at me suspiciously.

"Completely. I was drinking myself to death," I said. "I was chain smoking and stuffing myself with all the wrong foods, not sleeping, not taking care of my body on any level. I didn't understand then, just like you don't understand now, that I didn't need to die. That I could live a normal, healthy, happy life if I took care of myself the right way. If I stopped doing the harmful things and started doing the helpful things, starting with these."

I held out an orange plastic prescription bottle of AZT, a week's supply. "You take this every day," I said. "Make sure you follow the instructions exactly. It's very important not to miss a dose. If you do, you risk giving the disease a window to grow stronger. I won't lie to you, the first few weeks will be hard. The side effects can be terrible. But they will fade, you just have to give it time. Remember—Anthony and I are never more than a phone call away. Padre Antonio always knows how to reach us."

"Life is a gift, Alberto," Anthony said. "You can make the most of yours, whether or not you tell your parents."

When Alberto rose to leave, Padre Antonio followed him to the door and put his arms around the boy awkwardly. Anthony raised his eyebrow in my direction. The padre was trying. Before we left that morning, Padre Antonio thanked us over and over again, giving us real hugs and several kisses on both cheeks. It was like he didn't quite know how else to show his gratitude, other than through longer hugs and more kisses. We got the message that our help was appreciated.

February came and went. After our extraordinary night at the New Year's Eve festivities, I wanted to dance every chance I got. Anthony tried to keep pace with me, and although he was decidedly not a terrific dancer, he had fun.

For Anthony, the most important thing was always that we got enough rest, ate well, took care of ourselves, and kept up to date on the best treatment options for HIV. I had him pretty well convinced that dance counted as an excellent form of healthy exercise, and that made him feel better about all the revelry we were indulging in. It was such a happy time for us, that summer in Florianopolis. Even if we didn't get the barraca put up until afternoon, who cared? Most of our beach customers didn't show up until noon, either.

The one thing that did detract from my overall glee was Padre Antonio's obvious suffering. He loved both Anthony and me, that much was impossible not to see, and he was sincerely grateful for our help with his work with HIV victims, and yet, it was also plain that he was struggling on some level. It was as if he was always holding something back, and I was pretty sure I knew what it was. After all, no matter how helpful or good or kind we were, wasn't it still true that at the end of the day, Anthony and I were sinners in the eyes of the Church? One morning in early March, after a meeting with a very terrified, very miserable nineteen-year-old named Pablo, whose HIV had unfortunately advanced already into some early AIDS symptoms, I decided to act on my hunch. "Is it hard for you, Padre?" I asked.

"It's excruciating, yes," he said. "To see these young men suffer. I don't know what I would do without you."

"No, not just them," I said. "Me. Anthony. Is it hard for you to witness our work with you and your congregation, when we are sinners in the eyes of your church?"

Padre Antonio sat down and let out a long, slow sigh. He motioned for me to sit back down, too. Neither of us spoke. When Padre finally broke the silence, his voice boomed overly loud in the still room. "You were created in God's image," he said. "And everything that God does is perfect. You and Anthony are full of love, love for each other, love for everyone you serve, and love for the frightened young men you are counseling."

"And still, we are sinners," I challenged. "To be condemned."

In a soft voice, the padre continued: "I have always been a devout Catholic and have believed and preached the encyclical Humanae Vitae—the doctrine of human life. It reaffirms the Church's stance against birth control, and the belief that the sexual act must retain its intrinsic relationship to the procreation of human life. Furthermore, I've been taught that homosexual sex is a sin, and that therefore gays must live their lives in celibacy."

"So that's what you believe?"

"The fact of the matter is that most of my parishioners don't believe this doctrine and even those who do don't seem to follow it. Every day in the confessional, I hear about the many forms of birth control, the loss of virginity, the affairs, the promiscuous sex. When John Paul II became Pope in 1978, he affirmed the Humane Vitae but he also said—," here Padre pulled some papers from a folder and read, "Christ has not come to judge the world but to save it, and while he was uncompromisingly stern towards sin, he was patient and rich in mercy towards sinner."

I said nothing.

"I know a thing or two about celibacy," he said. "Officially, it is seen as a higher state than married life, an exalted state of virginity. So from that point of view, it is hard for me to consider celibacy for gays as an imposition, when in fact it is an invitation to a higher calling."

"And you really believe this?" I asked. "You don't see the hypocrisy in it? The contradiction in how it's fine for married people to have sex way past the age of childbearing—that's not for procreation. There's so much bullshit in all this—forgive me for the profanity. But it makes me angry, Padre."

"Listen, Bruno," he said. "Never in all my seventy years have I questioned my Pope or my Church doctrine. But since you and Anthony showed up, I've been—well, let's just say I haven't had a moment of peace. I think part of what's preying on me, if I'm to be fully honest with you, is the loneliness of my own life. I've sacrificed the opportunity for human intimacy, a sacrifice I made willingly at the time, because I believed so fully in the doctrine. And it is true that being of service to my parishioners has been a joy and a balm. But is it true that the service and the celibacy are inexorably linked? I think of Paul in Corinthians, saying it is better to marry than to burn. But if the fundamentals my vows were based upon were not as infallible as I once believed, or if my beliefs change, then has my own life not been what I thought it was?"

He didn't wait for my answer, not that I had one. "My main issue," he continued, "when it comes right down to it, is that the New Testament is about Jesus. It's about Jesus, Bruno. About the Messiah, whose message was a message of love."

"But not sexual love between men," I countered, even though I knew I wasn't exactly on point with the padre's line of reasoning. My aim was to push him into the thick of whatever was really bothering him about collaborating with Anthony and me. I wanted to go straight into the fire of it.

"Have I ever told you about Andre?" Padre asked. "He was the first baby I ever baptized when I moved here twenty-four years ago. Can you imagine that—the feeling that washes over you when you baptize a child in front of the congregation, when you give that infant to God? Andre's mother was a seamstress in Florianopolis. Still is, in fact. If you have need of sewing work, her skill is above all others. But I digress. The point is that she just about burst with pride when little Andre completed catechism and had his first communion. She was on her own by then because Andre's father, a fisherman, was killed in a storm when Andre was only three years old. I think often about Andre, who followed in his father's footsteps and became a fisherman. After a good day on the water, he would come by the parish with a big smile and his biggest catch for us to eat. And he showed up for Mass almost every Sunday with his mother. He was a light in her life—and to be honest, in mine, too."

"And now he has AIDS," I interrupted, sure that my guess about where this story was leading was exactly right.

"No. Now he is dead." The words hung between us. "Andre is dead. Just a few weeks before you and Anthony knocked on my door, I gave Andre his last rites. This, after watching him waste away from the terrible, unspeakable illness which his dear mother refused to acknowledge or admit. AIDS of course—though that was never said out loud. Not by him, by me, by his mother, by anyone. I had a strong suspicion that Andre was gay, but I could never have that conversation with him. I was afraid I would say all the wrong things."

"You would have found the right things to say, Padre."

"If you could see my doubts, you might think differently. Frankly, you have neither the devoutness nor the theological comprehension necessary to understand my qualms. This entire conversation is inappropriate in the highest degree, and I realize that. Just the fact that I am sitting here, saying these things to you, is indicative of how lost I am. And how can this be? I have been a faithful priest for forty years. And yet, the more I've prayed about this, the more upset and confused I've become. And in that state, I am supposed to give counsel and support to these frightened young men and their families? I think of Andre and the joy he missed in his short life, and I wonder. Why? Simply because he did not have the call to celibacy, a free gift from God as I received, this good, devout boy who I knew since birth was forced to choose either to sin or to live a lonely, solitary life? I cannot believe it had to be that way. And what if you and Anthony had been here to reach out to him? This, Bruno, is why you and Anthony are such a miracle for me. I wasn't able to do this work without you. Clarity still eludes me, but I can feel it drawing closer. I pray, Bruno. I pray and I pray."

"We all pray, Padre," I said. "In our own ways."

"Bruno, do me a favor. Meet me tomorrow night at the Velho Pescador for a late dinner. Bring Anthony. There's someone who needs to meet you."

The following evening, Anthony and I arrived at the Velho Pescador just as Padre Antonio had instructed. The maître d' led us through the dimly lit dining room—vintage chandeliers hung from the twelve-foot ceilings under which round, white-clothed tables were circled by finely dressed men and women whose chatter filled the space with echoes of cheer and anticipation. We were heading toward a table in the far corner of the room, next to the floor-to-ceiling window that overlooked the bay. Beside Padre Antonio sat a middle-aged man in a navy suit coat over a crisp, white shirt. His gray hair was tightly cropped to his head, and he wore round glasses that rested downward toward the end of his nose. Padre Antonio jumped to his feet when he saw us approaching. "Bruno, Anthony," he said. "Meet Dr. Osmar Pinto, a dear friend of mine."

"Hello, hello," said the doctor, half standing and nodding toward Anthony and me. "A pleasure to meet you."

He didn't look pleased, though. He looks slightly repelled, I thought. Anthony caught my eye, telling me in one quick glance that he picked up on the strangeness too.

"Sit down, sit down," Padre Antonio said, gesturing toward the maître d', who had pulled a chair back and was waiting for one of us to seat ourselves in it. I put my hand on Anthony's shoulder and invited him to sit first. The truth was that I wasn't sure how much I wanted to take a seat at this point, and yet I knew too that I was being irrational, letting the strange vibe from Dr. Osmar lead me to conclusions before there was anything concrete to conclude about.

The waiter poured our waters and brought wine for the table— apparently they had begun the order before we arrived—and Padre Antonio cleared his throat. "Gentlemen, it's wonderful you've come tonight. I believe you can help Dr. Osmar with a problem he has been wrestling with. I believe you are the only ones I know, in fact, who can be of real help in this situation." He looked at me meaningfully. Anthony kicked me under the table.

"Is this because we are gay?" I asked. Why not cut right to the chase, I thought, feeling the blood rise to my face. Padre Antonio had set us up, clearly, and without the decency of a warning let alone our overt permission. What was this going to be about?

"That, yes, and also—at least as much or more—because of your outstanding work with the men of my parish, the men afflicted with AIDS. I've told Dr. Osmar about what you have done for me and for the parishioners I was unable to help, and I think your compassion and your wisdom can be of great help to the doctor now as well, just as it was for me—."

"Which I appreciate," Dr. Osmar cut in. "I really do. But I must admit, I'm skeptical. This is a situation that, frankly, has no solution." Padre held the wine bottle, a bright Cabernet, above my glass.

"Yes, thank you," I said. It was still a rare thing for me to drink, but I felt wine would be needed for this situation.

Dr. Osmar continued. "The crux of the situation is simple and, I'm afraid to say, rather grim. The truth is I find it harder and harder to treat my gay patients and the number of them is increasing due to the HIV cases flowing into my practice."

"What exactly is it that you find difficult?" Anthony said. I was surprised at his jumping in this way, and at the edge in his voice. "After all, with the improved treatments now available, I would think treating your gay patients would be easier than ever."

"The drugs are not the problem," Dr. Osmar said. "All I can think of is how disgusting they are, what sexual perverts they are. Part of me thinks they deserve this punishment from God." He looked back and forth from Anthony to me as he spoke these words.

I swallowed the last of my wine. "Padre Antonio," I said. "Is this how you feel about your gay parishioners?" I paused and poured myself a generous second glass of wine, without looking to Anthony for his permission. "Is this," I continued, "how you feel about Anthony and me?"

"No. It is not. I have been giving this—as you know, Bruno— great thought and consideration. And I have arrived at this question. A question especially for you, Osmar. Think, if you will, please, of how you felt when you realized what your parents did with each other in order for you to be born. Ponder this act for a moment, don't shy from it. I know that I for one was in complete denial about this as a boy and even as a young man. I couldn't believe it for a moment that my parents would undertake such an act. Far easier, in fact, was to believe I was the product of a virgin birth."

Dr. Osmar and I laughed. But Anthony's face remained stony.

"You're right about that, Padre," Dr. Osmar said. "Disgust was the sensation I felt when I first realized this inevitable fact, utter disgust. Still a bit of disgust even now, just thinking of it." He laughed again, and shook his head. "And this is sanctioned sex we're discussing," he said. "Forbidden acts are yet another, altogether darker realm, are they not?"

"Well, we both know that forbidden sexual acts are not the exclusive domain of gay men," Padre Antonio said. Was that a knowing glance Padre Antonio had just shot the doctor? I caught Anthony's eye; he'd seen it, too! Something the old doctor had whispered in the confessional more than once, I had to wonder?

"I've given a lot of thought to this," Padre Antonio continued. "I'm seventy years old. I've studied the scriptures. I know what Paul wrote about two men who live together, just like Bruno and Anthony here."

Again, the blood rose to my face, and I didn't know if I was embarrassed or angry or both. But I did want to know what Padre was going to say next.

"But Paul could not have known what we know now, that some men have a homosexual orientation from birth. Science only uncovered that reality in the last fifty years. The church must adapt along with the world we live in."

The silence that enveloped our table was as thick as pudding, so dense that even the chattering and laughing of the rest of the restaurant couldn't seem to penetrate it. Fortunately the waiter arrived to take our orders, which siphoned off just enough of the tension to make it bearable. To my left, Anthony was so wired I thought he might actually just get up and leave the table if things continued this same path. I rested my hand on his thigh under the table and gave it a squeeze. Padre Antonio meant well, of that I was certain. We could do this.

As the waiter left the table with our orders, Padre Antonio continued. "I'm also a devout Catholic priest trying to understand how Jesus felt about this," he said. "His message is about love. He was also aware of sex during his time. In Matthew Jesus says, 'Not everyone can accept this teaching, but only those to whom it is given. For there are eunuchs who have been so from birth, and there are eunuchs who have been made eunuchs by others, and there are eunuchs who have made themselves eunuchs for the sake of the kingdom. Let everyone accept this who can.'"

"Padre," I said. "I won't pretend to have any real knowledge of scripture, or exactly how eunuchs relate to what we're discussing, but to me, that sounds like Jesus was preaching acceptance."

Dr. Osmar let out a snuffling scoff. "Eunuchs have nothing to do with homosexual deviance," he said.

"Yes, but in this scripture Jesus recognizes that someone may be born with sexual differences," Padre Antonio said. "And in homosexual cases, I believe a person could be born with an attraction to members of their own sex. According to Jesus they are accepted into the kingdom of God and are not doomed to hell."

"Thank you, Padre," I said. "That's what I was trying to get at before. It's right in the last comment, 'Let everyone accept this who can.'"

"And Jesus was also saying that it is hard to understand," Anthony said, again surprising me. "And that it's OK to struggle with accepting sexual differences, that's OK, but acceptance is the goal."

"What about Paul's teachings on the evils of homosexuality?" Dr. Osmar said.

"I wonder if Paul was not preaching about the Jewish laws rather than Jesus's teaching," Padre said. "He refers to same-sex acts as unclean and unnatural, but I cannot see anywhere he talks about homosexuality as sinful, punishable by eternal condemnation."

"Again, I don't know much, or anything at all, actually, about Jewish laws," I said, "but I do know there is no way that Anthony—a man who devotes his life to helping others and bringing love and goodness to the world—is going to be condemned to any kind of damnation, eternal or otherwise."

"My heart resonates with that," Padre said. "And I would say the same of you, Bruno. The truth is that things change and evolve. The teachings of the Church are not immune to that, and we must acknowledge that it is so, even when it's not easy or comfortable. In Corinthians, for example, Paul teaches that men are ahead of women, women must not speak in church, women must wear veils, and men must not have long hair. And that it's fine to have slaves."

"Don't you wonder," Anthony asked, "if we're not dealing with some man-made errors of translation in addition to the historical context in which these men were writing?"

Clearly, Anthony had paid better attention during the church service he attended in his youth than I had. We rarely discussed religion, and I had assumed his knowledge of Catholicism was like mine: half-formed and residual. Of course I should have known he would take the time to understand something, especially if he did not agree with it.

"Again, I come back to Jesus," Padre said, "and his teachings of forgiveness and unconditional love. For the life of me I can't see Jesus not loving and accepting most of the homosexual persons I have met and counseled—including Bruno and Anthony."

Dr. Osmar lowered his head. "I think you are treading on very dangerous ground, Padre," he said. I felt Anthony stiffen in his chair. "You're questioning the teachings of the Church."

"I'm finished," Anthony said icily. "I've tried to show patience but this crosses my line." He started to rise and I followed his lead, but Dr. Osmar held up both hands. "Sit, sit down," he said. "Let me finish. Though I am deeply uncomfortable with this line of reasoning, I cannot find a way to argue or disagree with any of you on these points. Clearly I have to do a lot more thinking and praying. There is a lot more to talk about. More thoughts to share. But tonight let us, four men equal in God's eyes, enjoy our dinner together. Please."

CHAPTER SIXTEEN

The Greatest Show on Earth

One morning, which began just like any other morning, I realized we were three days into February. January was over, and that meant Carnaval was just around the corner. I dug out a calendar— Easter fell on April 7, and since Carnaval takes place 40 days before Easter, the exact day this year would be February 20. Festivities would begin the week before and last until Ash Wednesday. I couldn't believe I had less than a month to prepare, especially considering this would be Anthony's first Brazilian Carnaval. If I had anything to say about it, it would be one he would never forget. I hoped I had time to do all that I wanted to do.

It was a Saturday, bright and breezy. Some eager beach goers had already set up on the sand when we arrived. It would be a busy day, but I couldn't delay preparations any longer.

"Your hair looks fantastic today," I said, leaning my head into the space between Anthony's shoulder blades.

"That's funny, considering I woke up late this morning and skipped my shower," he replied.

"You're working the grunge look. It's hot."

He turned to face me. "OK, what's up?"

"I don't know if I should answer that in public," I said with a smirk.

"Bruno, what's gotten into you?"

"Carnaval!"

"Carna . . . isn't that at the end of February? Or do you do things differently in Brazil?"

"We definitely do things differently, but yes, it is at the end of February. February 20, to be exact. So I have seventeen days to get everything ready."

"Seventeen days? You'll need that long? What exactly is this 'everything' you're getting ready?"

"I'm still figuring that out! As soon as I do, you'll be the first to know."

Anthony shook his head bemusedly. "I'll hold down the fort here. You get going on all that 'everything.'"

I took the camioneta and headed to town. As I drove, I made a mental list of everything I would need: wide elastic bands, glue, strong threads, and most essentially, as many colorful feathers as I could get my hands on. Though I hadn't yet bought a single thing on the list, I was already impatient to begin designing and constructing our costumes. It didn't take long to find everything I needed. Car full of feathers, and head full of sketches, I headed back to Joaquim Beach.

Anthony whistled when he saw my haul. "No wonder you need over two weeks! We celebrate Carnaval in Venezuela, too, but I don't remember this many feathers being involved."

"It's not just feathers," I said. "Carnaval is by far the biggest holiday in Brazil. Real life literally stops. The entire week leading up to Ash Wednesday, it's only parades, parties, dancing, celebrating. The biggest parties are in Rio, but all Brazilian cities take part. Florianopolis may not have the numbers of other cities, but we have spirit. You'll see."

"You really celebrate for a whole week? We really only celebrated the two days before Ash Wednesday. My favorite part was always the water fights. Even adults get in on it, throwing water balloons and shooting squirt guns at passersby and cars."

"I hope you're ready for some grown-up fun this year," I said. "Now, let me describe what I'm imagining for our costumes."

The color theme was the Brazilian national colors: green, yellow, and blue. We needed two costumes: one to wear while working at the beach, and a more elaborate one for parties. For work, I envisioned Speedos covered in blue feathers. "We can glue them in place, then sew them down to really secure them," I explained. "I think that's better than using staples. Too uncomfortable, and too easy to detach."

"I don't even know how to thread a needle," Anthony said,"but I should be able to handle the gluing, if you give me a quick tutorial."

After we had the Speedos bedecked to my satisfaction, I turned my attention to our headdresses. For these, I had purchased 12-inch long yellow and green feathers. For the parties, we would add wear bands of those foot-long feathers in yellow, green, and blue around our upper arms and upper legs. Both the headdresses and the arm and leg bands could be made using the same technique: first gluing, then sewing the feathers onto 2-inch wide elastic bands.

While we worked on our costumes, I gave Anthony a crash course on Carnaval traditions in Brazil, and more specifically, in Florianopolis. "There are four basic settings," I said. "First, Carnaval on the beach. They bring out extra-loud speakers and blare samba music from sun-up until early morning. You'll see people dancing almost around the clock."

"No wonder you're so excited," Anthony said, as he pulled bits of blue feather fluff from the glue residue stuck to his fingers.

"The serious dancing doesn't happen on the beaches, though. That takes place at the Sambadrome. Rio had the first and the largest, of course, but all the major cities have their own now. The Sambadrome here in Florianopolis was inaugurated in 1989."

"Let me guess, the Sambadrome is for . . . samba-ing?"

"Aren't you a clever one! Basically it's an alleyway with bleachers and box seats on both sides. The samba schools and floats parade between them to be seen and judged. Did I tell you my father was in a samba school once? In Rio, no less!"

"I'm sure that's very impressive, but in order to appreciate it, I'll need you to enlighten me on the subject of 'samba schools.'"

"Samba schools are, well, they're like neighborhood dance groups. They spend the entire year planning and perfecting the themes of the dances, costumes, and floats. Each school keeps their plans secret so the debut at the 'greatest show on earth'—the carnival parade—will be as dramatic as possible. Anyway, about, oh, maybe ten years ago, my dad spent $450 to be part of a Rio samba school."

"He spent $450? To be in a parade?"

"Not just—it included his costume, and you're dancing with

hundreds or even thousands of dancers in front of this massive crowd. I can't even imagine the rush. Today I think it would cost $1,000 or more."

"Please don't tell me you're working on a last-minute enrollment."

"No, no, like I said, they practice all year! But I did order us first class seats for the Sambadrome. We'll have to go to my dad's yacht club, too. That's another Carnaval setting, the private clubs. He'll probably be at this club for most of the week. Personally I think it's a little stuffy. You will see some of the most elaborate costumes there, because——."

"Cha-ching," Anthony said.

"Exactly. So we'll show up, say hello, and you can try to guess how much each outfit cost. Then we'll move on to my favorite part of Carnaval—the street. All the streets next to the central park are closed to traffic and packed with thousands and thousands of people. Everyone wears costumes, though not everyone's will be as good as ours. We'll dance and sing the night away. It's going to be a whirlwind. Oh, and remind me to point out the *Desfile do Bloco dos Sujos* to you."

"They're called . . . the Dirty Group Parade?"

I laughed. "Not a bad translation! They're a group of men who dress as women."

"So, drag queens."

"Not quite. They say they're 'getting in touch with their feminine side,' but there's sort of a homophobic attitude among many of them. Like, by dressing that way, they're ridiculing any man who might really want to get in touch with his feminine side."

Reflecting on Carnaval, as I introduced Anthony to its intricate customs, I realized what I loved most was the underlying attitude of anything goes. The rules of daily life were erased so that even the nicest of nice girls felt free to wear glittering costumes that revealed more than they concealed. Carnaval is the last chance for fun before the lean days of Lent.

One thing I forgot to mention to Anthony was an old Brazilian drug called *lança-perfume*. In my wild days, and I had certainly been in the midst of those when I attended my last Carnaval, I hadn't given it a second thought. But the new, clean me had a different take on lança-perfume. It scared me.

Anthony actually spotted one of the telltale bottles before I did. "What are those?" he asked.

"Careful!" I shouted. Then, leaning close to him and lowering my voice: "Those are filled with a drug called lança-perfume. Sometimes they start spraying everyone within range."

"I'll keep my distance," he said, then, "It's still so cute to me when you go all D.A.R.E."

Lança-perfume is best known as part of the mayhem of Carnaval. Inhaling gives you a quick hit of euphoria. It had actually been outlawed in the 1960s, though that had done little to deter enthusiasts. Chemically speaking, lança-perfume contains a mix of ether, chloroform, ethyl chloride, and a scent. The scent is crucial to cover the foul odor of the chemicals, especially the ether. Because it comes in aerosol bottles, it can be sprayed into the faces of those around you, whether they consent or not. Despite the best efforts of the police, the little bottles were still everywhere during Carnaval.

I understood the appeal, but I could no longer disregard the downsides as I once had. The short-lived high could turn dangerous, from a loss of feeling in your legs to potentially fatal disruptions of your heartbeat. Some people are more susceptible than others, of course, but there's no way to find out whether you will be before you try it. People doing just that keep the hospital emergency rooms extra busy during Carnaval. I had never experienced anything more unpleasant than some dizziness and shakes, and I didn't intend to push my luck.

The only high either of us indulged in that day came from being part of a throng of merrymakers. Still, when I woke up the next morning—or more accurately, afternoon—I had a popular 1980s song commemorating the joys of lança-perfume running through my head. I sang a few snatches under my breath as I surreptitiously wriggled the fingers of my right hand. Anthony had slept with my arm wrapped around him, and now that arm was very much asleep. He rolled over to face me, and I took the opportunity to shift my arm out from under him.

"What's that you're singing?" he asked, still half asleep so his words slurred sweetly together.

"An old love song," I said, laughing a little. "A love song about lança-perfume."

He groaned in mock exasperation and buried his face in the crook of my neck.

"What did you think of Brazilian Carnaval?" I asked, petting his hair.

I felt him take a deep breath. After a pause, he said, "To tell you the truth, I'm glad it only happens once a year, and I'm glad it only happens in Brazil. No, don't get defensive! I can feel you tensing up. I just mean I don't think the rest of the world could survive! Even though you prepared me for what was to come, I thought you had to be exaggerating. No description could convey what I just experienced. I don't know if I could survive it again!"

∿

Chapter Seventeen

Arrivals and Departures

June finally blew in on the cold winds from Antarctica, and the tourists blew out almost overnight, leaving a deserted stretch of beach in their wake. The winter rainy season would persist until October. We had several months before the beaches would come alive again with happy vacationers. This quiet season meant that Anthony and I would finally, finally have time for a real vacation of our own. "Not a moment too soon!" he said when I announced this early one morning. "I loved the barraca, but man, we need a break," he said. And he was right. We both desperately needed relief from the long hours we'd been working all summer.

I also wanted to show Anthony as much as I could of my beloved home country. If I shared the best of it with him, I hoped he would come to love it as much as I did. It was as if, in a way, I was trying to bring Anthony back in time with me to the years before I knew him, sharing the most important elements of my life before he was in it. We went first to Brasilia where we could just unwind and shake off the tension of the summer beach season. After a few days there, we headed to Belem, a large city located at the mouth of the Amazon River and the Atlantic Ocean. From there, we traveled by boat to Manaus, the capital city of the state of Amazon. This was something I myself had never done, and I relished the adventure. I'd always wanted to take the trip from Belem to Manaus by boat, and bringing Anthony along for the ride was truly icing on the cake.

"It'll be so nice to be literally 'in the same boat' with you," Anthony said. "You're a fantastic guide, but it's almost more fun for us both to be tourists." Though all the boats were referred to as *gaiolas*, or bird cages, some were only fitted with hammocks for passengers to sleep on, while others also featured a few small private cabins. After some searching, I found a boat with a vacant cabin. I reserved the space on the *D'Jard Viera* immediately.

I never dreamt it would be such an odyssey.

The *D'Jard Viera* was scheduled to leave at noon the following day. Anthony and I were some of the first passengers to board. Despite the announced hour of departure, we did not pull out of the port until around 8 p.m. which, I told Anthony, was a sure indicator we were running on true Brazilian time now. Our tiny cabin had no windows and no adjoining bathroom, though we did have the luxury of a noisy yet functional air conditioner.

Each day, the meals were the same. For breakfast, we had crackers, butter, coffee, and hot chocolate. For lunch and dinner, rice or pasta, beans, and some kind of meat—often a freshly caught fish. There were about sixty passengers total, many of whom we became quite friendly with over the course of the trip. We spent the majority of our social time with a Jesuit priest on his way to

Manaus and a young anthropologist who was using his sabbatical to study Amazonian culture. Both were great conversationalists and ruthless card sharks, especially when it came to bridge.

As our boat navigated the tributaries of the Amazon leading to Manaus, we stopped in various cities to deliver and pick up passengers and goods. From the hammocks on the top deck, we had a full view of all the goings-on. Every time we neared a city or town, small boats steered by women and children would flock to us, their crews begging for donations. Passengers on our boat would toss them clothing, food, and any other personal items they could spare.

We finally arrived in Manaus on Saturday afternoon. The trip flew by so much faster than I had imagined, especially with our many stops and our newfound friends. Nonetheless, both of us were glad to place our feet on solid ground.

It was exhilarating for me to experience the newness of these lush and dramatic surroundings in the exact same fresh, overpowering way that Anthony was. I liked the way it felt to share each spate of planning and deciding, to be shocked by nature, and to clear each hurdle together. "I've never felt closer to you, Bruno," Anthony said one morning in Manaus. I had just prepared our coffee, which we'd brought outside to the patio, and the sun was just a sliver above the horizon in the east. There was not another soul in sight, so obviously I leaned across the small metal tabletop and kissed him long and hard. Life was so good.

From Manaus we took a smaller boat up the Rio Negro and spent several days camping out in the deep Amazon jungles. We fished for piranhas, and hunted and caught small crocodiles. We also had a number of close encounters with extraordinarily large and—I have to admit this, though I wouldn't at the time—terrifying snakes. When Anthony said he felt more virile than ever, I thought at first he was poking fun at the scenario I'd put us in, but by the look on his face, he was clearly sincere. "I'm just bursting with life," he said. "I feel like the whole world is flowing through my veins." Nothing is like the Amazon jungle; it is an otherworldly place. Even the ants were six times the size of their more ordinary cousins.

The dense green that surrounded us had a presence beyond what we could see. It was a green that you breathed right into your lungs with every inhale, a green you tasted and smelled. "I feel," Anthony said one night as we were settling to sleep in our tent, "as if the green is seeping into me. Becoming part of me. Subtly changing me for the better, you know?" I did know. What he said was exactly what I was feeling: a sense of total immersion in and connection to nature that I couldn't explain but that filled me with peace and a sense of oneness with the world. It was more powerful than anything I'd ever felt in church, to be honest.

After our time in the jungle, we spent our last three days in Manaus. Anthony wanted to see the historic opera house, built in 1881 during the great Amazon rubber boom. "This is the opera house in Fitzcarraldo!" Anthony told me.

My face indicated what that meant to me: exactly nothing.

"Oh, you know the one," he said, "about the guy who goes through such a miserable journey to finally get to hear Caruso sing?" When we got there, he let slip that there was no proof that Caruso ever actually sang in the Manaus Opera House. "Who cares?" he quickly added. "It adds to the intrigue of the story. I, for one, can easily imagine it being true. Besides, it's a conversation piece. Don't be a spoilsport."

From Manaus we went back to Itajai, where my dad was also spending time. I was anxious to see him. He hadn't been doing well since retiring, which he'd done shortly after my mother died. His spark had gone out, it seemed. I had especially noticed this during the New Year's Eve celebrations. He'd looked just as sharp as always, but right beneath the appearance of his old self was something sorrowful and empty. I had observed him carefully through the course of that otherwise joyous evening, and came away with the thought that he was drained. He barely sang or danced, and he had exuded little joy or excitement when observing the singing and dancing of others. He was going through the motions, but his heart wasn't in it.

Anthony easily agreed that we'd spend the rest of the winter in Itajai to be closer to my dad. The other reason to stay in Itajai was to get a start on my latest business idea, which was to design and produce t-shirts depicting different views of Joaquim Beach. I wanted to show the majesty of the surf and capture the stark beauty of the sand and ocean. Most of all I wanted my paintings to be alive with color and action, with the pulsating humanity that made Joaquim Beach what it was. Itajai was a great city for the project, because vendors were plentiful and prices were moderate. I contacted a textile firm, chose the best quality of cotton fabric, and ordered a thousand shirts of various sizes printed with my hand-painted designs. When I'd approved the completed shirts, I had them sent to Armacao. Anthony and I would sell them for top dollar when we hit the beach again next season.

My father agreed to return with us to Armacao in November. He had a project he wanted to complete on the house there— expanding the patio and putting in a guesthouse and swimming pool. I was thrilled because such a large project would give my father something to look forward to, something to immerse himself in, something to re-ignite his enthusiasm.

The first week of December we were back on the beach, and our barraca was loaded with my custom t-shirts. We couldn't believe how fast they flew out of our hands. In less than a month I had to re-order all the designs in every size. Now we had two solid sources of income, and as one sunny day folded into the next, life just seemed to get better and better. Ironically, though, in spite of our success in Brazil, I found myself thinking more and more about Miami, and when we might return. Betty, Rosa, the fitness center, all of it was showing up in my dreams more and more often.

"When was the last time you called Betty?" Anthony wanted to know one evening, as if he'd read my mind. I was chopping shallots for a white sauce. The kitchen smelled heavenly.

"I don't know—well, I mean, on her birthday, October 12, for sure I called her then," I said. Only in saying it out loud did I realize what a long time ago that was. I was planning to call her on Christmas, as I always did. I wanted to be sure Betty never felt alone during the holidays. She continued to show nothing but generosity and kindness toward me even now, when our situation had transformed so radically from what she must have long ago imagined our married life together would be. My lifesaver, I liked to call her. I would always be indebted to Betty. I should show her how much I loved her more often, I thought. Why did I have to reserve phone calls for holidays and special occasions? I didn't, was the answer.

"You don't need to wait until Christmas, Bruno." Anthony did this often, the mind reading thing, except his conscience was always more rigorous, more demanding than my own. "I've been meaning to check in with Betty myself. Do you know if that Venezuelan couple is still renting the condo?"

"Yes, but only until March. They're expecting a baby, apparently. Buying a house, she thought."

"Well, then, now we need to call," Anthony said. "Hopefully she can get another renter in right away, but if not, we're going to have to rework our budget."

"I'm not worried about covering the rent," I said, "especially with the t-shirt sales going the way they are. It would be worth it to me to put most of our profits toward paying the rent ourselves, if that's what we have to do to stay here." Funny how a moment ago I'd been day dreaming about when we'd resume life back in Miami, but now I was arguing that we'd pay rent for an empty condo in order to stay in Brazil.

"Your father?" Anthony said.

Bingo. My father, my worry for him, was the source of my confusion. Did I want to stay in Brazil to look after him, or was I afraid to? "I'm glad he's nearby now, but it's hard to see the ways he's not himself, even with his construction projects. I'm not sure how to help."

"Maybe you should talk to Rosa."

"What can Rosa do all the way from Miami?"

"Stubborn," said Anthony. "You're just so stubborn. It doesn't have to be from Miami. Rosa could visit. She hasn't been down once since we left Miami—and it's been more than a year."

"You're right," I said. "Always right." I turned from the skillet and grabbed him under the chin and kissed him. "I'll call Rosa tonight when we get home from the church."

At that very moment the telephone rang, and when I lifted the receiver I couldn't believe what I heard: "Hello? *Olá*? Do I have the right number? My name is Betty, I'm looking for Bruno, is he there? Um . . . Bruno's casa? Or do you know an Anthony?"

I was so startled to hear her voice, it took me a minute to reply. She was never the one to call, and my immediate thought was that something must be wrong, but that didn't compute, either, because her "hello" sounded so happy. "Betty! It's me, it's Bruno. Sorry to leave you hanging, but I could hardly believe it was you! We were just talking about you! Is everything OK?"

"Better than OK! Bruno, what would you say if Rosa and I came to Brazil right after New Year's?"

"Oh my God, you can't know—I can't begin to tell you, in fact—how truly miraculous that would be. But the tickets, the time off work, how can you swing it? And wait, back up, you and Rosa?"

"Well, I was over at Rosa's last night for dinner—."

"You voluntarily went to my sister's for dinner? All on your own?"

"She was having a dinner for Ricardo and Beth and the baby—."

"Baby? As in, Ricardo's baby? My brother is a father?"

"Bruno, for someone who loves to talk, you're terrible at staying in touch. Yes, Ricardo's baby, and Beth's, you know, Ricardo's girlfriend—have you even met her?"

"Beth? That sounds so wholesome. I'm sure I would remember if Ricardo introduced me to a Beth."

"She's wonderful, Bruno, beyond wonderful. I just adore her, and Rosa does too. Something we agree on! She's great for Ricardo, too. I can't believe you haven't met her. Have you really been away so long? But anyway, she had the baby August 15. He's the most beautiful little boy, baby Marco, he's called. As handsome as your brother. And he actually looked beautiful right away, not all smushed and blotchy. I mean, all babies come out a little blotchy—wait, this isn't even why I called. I have news!"

"More news? Betty, I'm already overwhelmed!"

"Well, just you wait because Papa Ricardo gave me the most wonderful early Christmas present: a round trip ticket to Brazil, for whenever I want to go. He's sending Rosa too. He says he'll stay in Miami for a change, and help Luigi and the rest of them deal with the fitness center and the whole frenzy of the New Year's resolution crowd this year."

I laughed, too giddy to put together a complete thought. "This is all ridiculously exciting, Betty. I can hardly believe it's happening. I have to make Anthony pinch me. He's going to flip! Let me know the instant you book your flights."

"I will. I need to start thinking about that, and a million other things, too. Not to mention getting my Brazilian visa underway."

As soon as I set the phone back in its cradle, I flung my arms around Anthony and spun us around the kitchen until we tipped over onto the floor in a heap. "Betty's coming," I told him, using one arm to prop myself up so I could see his face.

"I gathered," he said.

I sank back against him, letting my body relax into his. I pressed my face into the curve of his neck and tucked one hand reassuringly under his ribcage. "Rosa, too," I mumbled. "Do you think this is God's way of saying 'Thank you'? Oh, and speaking of, we better go."

"Go?" Anthony cupped my ass and pulled my hips firmly into his.

I rocked up to my knees, his body straddled by my thighs. "We're on our way to church, remember?"

He groaned. "We give plenty of our time to the church. God will understand if we skip, just this once."

"Not today," I said. "A kid from Palhoca is coming up to see Padre. The word is spreading all the way to Joiville about our work, access to medicines, all of it. I told you about all of this yesterday, you know, this is the kid who sounds like a real desperate case. Padre's not sure he's got much time left, but he wants us to help if we can. Padre doesn't want to counsel this one on his own."

For the most part, Padre felt comfortable talking to the young men now, but this time, he had told me, he was truly unsure of how much or whether he could help. Plus, there was something else he wanted to talk to us about—a young prostitute in his congregation had apparently become pregnant, and for some reason I couldn't quite grasp, Padre was especially worked up about it. I didn't want to be callous, but I couldn't help thinking, don't prostitutes get pregnant all the time?

"Maria," Padre said, as we sat in his office awaiting the young man from Palhoca. "It takes all my strength simply to say her name out loud to you. She is the most horrible secret I have, and the bloodiest."

Anthony and I sat in the wooden chairs across from Padre's desk and waited for him to continue. In the cool of his office, the scent of wood polish heavy in the air, I was keenly aware of what Anthony and I had got up to in the kitchen right before church. It felt life-giving and good, and I didn't want it to dissipate in this shadowy chill.

"I knew all along she was a troubled soul," Padre said. "Every New Year's Eve she would dress in her long white dress, one she designed and made herself from her own bed linens. She would carry a basket of fresh flowers and dance on the beach with the other local women, throwing her flowers into the waves as a gift to Rainha do Mar, Queen of the Sea. You know this ritual, Bruno." He looked more through me than at me, as if the scene was playing just behind my head.

"Some of the women make elaborate wooden boats to carry the flowers," he continued. "They all pray for the Rainha to care for the fishermen and provide for their well-being and prosperity."

"I love that ritual," I said. "I took Anthony to see it last year. It's full of such hope and joy. You can just feel the goodness of prayer rolling out on the waves."

"There is nothing joyful or good about Maria's prayers, let me assure you of that," Padre said, the words squeezing out bitterly between his closed teeth." Maria prayed for something sinister. She was convinced that the Queen would be happy to have a newborn baby's soul, the soul of her child, smothered there in the sand dunes. She believed that once she sacrificed her baby and prayed her special prayers, all would be perfect. Her baby would live forever with the Rainha."

Anthony looked sick. "That's disgusting," he said. "How could any mother do that? Bury her baby under the sand." He shuddered. I threaded my arm through his and nestled it close to my side.

"That baby's blood will always be on my hands," Padre said quietly. His hands were now folded in his lap, leathery and rough. He was unnaturally still and so, in turn, were we. He stared past us, still focused on something we couldn't see. I glanced at Anthony, and for the first time, though it must have been there since he shaved early that morning, I noticed a small cut on the left side of his chin, just a smear of dried blood now, really. For the longest time, no one spoke. It was me, of course, who finally broke the silence. I just couldn't stand it anymore. "Padre," I said, "you can't take responsibility for the actions of your congregants, no matter how terrible they may be. That is simply too much burden for you to bear."

"No," he said. He held up the palm of his hand in such a way that it seemed inordinately heavy, as if it had taken great strength for him to heft its weight from his lap. "If only that were true. But it's not. Maria talked openly about her plans to bury the child. I could have stopped her. I should have stopped her. But I did not. Her friends tried to talk her out of her terrible plans, but she was too deranged to listen. When she became pregnant a second time, she again talked freely of giving a second gift to the Queen of the Sea. I knew the second baby would be buried in the sand dunes, just as the first had been. This time, I tried my best to get her to change her mind, but she wouldn't budge. That was when I should have heard God's call more clearly. I should have intervened more forcefully, saved its life. But I was too cowardly to see that sometimes we must sin in order to serve God. Instead, I took what I saw as the easy path. How wrong I was. Easy it is not. Anything but. I took the path of darkness haunted by the screams of infants and visions of my own hands covered in their blood."

A sudden knock at the door made us all jump in our chairs. "I'm so sorry to interrupt," said Marta, peeking her dark head into the room. "The young man from Palhoca has yet to arrive, but I feel quite unwell. I'm afraid I need to lie down."

"Of course, Marta," Padre said, rising slowly from his chair and crossing to the door to press her hands between his. "I can listen for the door. Rest and be well, my child." Padre eased himself back into his chair, and I realized perhaps for the first time that he was an old man—a frail man.

"Padre," I said before he could start speaking again. "You need to stop beating yourself up. As terrible as this story is, what could you really have done to stop Maria? I know damn well you did your best—and what's done is done. It's in the past now."

"I still feel more guilt rests on my shoulders than you claim, and now I am to be tested again," Padre said. "For the last three years I have prayed every day for Maria. More than anything else, I have prayed that she would never get pregnant again. But now I am told by the midwife that she's carrying another child, and just as she did before, she is ranting about the Queen of the Sea. She will give birth in February or March." He stopped and put his face in his hands, then looked up again and continued. "I cannot endure the blood of another infant on my hands."

He looked from me to Anthony. "Sons, this gruesome crime is mine, not yours. But just as you have helped me to ease the suffering of the young men in Florianopolis who are suffering of HIV, you might be able to help me atone this sin, as well. The time is not yet come for me to say more. All I ask of you now is to hold this unborn infant in your hearts and in your prayers while I seek guidance from God on how to save them."

The young man from Palhoca never did arrive.

CHAPTER EIGHTEEN

Our Own Family

Christmas and New Year's came and went faster than ever. Not only was it our busiest time of the year on the beach, made even more complex now with managing the t-shirt inventory and sales, but we were also living every single moment of every day in anticipation of Betty's and Rosa's visit. My list of things we had to do and see during their stay was growing out of control, and Anthony had to keep reminding me, every time I ticked off another series of plans and events, that Betty would be with us for only ten days. "And what about Padre Antonio?" Anthony wanted to know when I regaled him for the millionth time with yet another jammed itinerary for the visit. "Where does that meeting fit on the agenda?"

"I decided not to introduce Betty to Padre Antonio," I said. "For his sake. I mean, I've never—we've never mentioned a wife in this complicated picture. Padre has come a long way, but that's just too much to ask from him, don't you think?"

"It doesn't feel right to leave her out," Anthony said. "We would be excluding her from such a crucial part of our lives here. But I see your point. It would probably be distressing to them both if we arranged an introduction."

When the day finally came, January 8, we packed it in early to head for the airport where we could watch their evening flight arrive. We hung out on the outside deck and clapped as we saw the airplane descending from the clouds. Together, we raced down the stairs to Gate 4. A few minutes later, out came Betty and Rosa, beaming at us with their arms wide open. We hugged and kissed them all the way to the luggage area. Soon we were on our way to Armacao.

Betty couldn't stop talking, so much so that Rosa had a hard time getting a word in. The trip to our house was only thirty minutes, thanks to the freshly paved road connecting the airport to Florianopolis. But instead of taking them straight back to the cottage, we veered off toward the ocean. As we crested a hill overlooking Armacao Beach, Betty exclaimed out loud.

"Oh, please stop! I have to take a picture," she said. "I just have to—it's breathtaking."

I think Betty might have stayed there snapping away until the sun set completely. "Come on Betty," Rosa finally insisted. "We can come back if you want more." She was anxious to get to our father's. She hadn't seen him since the barbecue for Betty's housewarming.

When we pulled up in Armacao, Dad and Matilda were waiting for us outside. Before I had even properly parked the car, Rosa bolted up the driveway into their arms. For the visit, Rosa would stay with Matilda, while Dad, Betty, and I stayed in the main house, and Anthony in the newly finished guesthouse. What no one aside from

Betty and Anthony seemed to notice—or at least they pretended not to—was that I spent my nights in the guesthouse as well.

Betty knew just enough Portuguese words to get along: *muito obrigada* (thank you); *bom dia, boa tarde,* and *boa noite* (good morning, good afternoon, and good night); and *sim* and *nao* (yes and no). She used what she knew as often as possible, which endeared her to my family and the other islanders.

Her presence also seemed to endear Anthony to them. I noticed that my uncles and aunts, the older generation, became a lot friendlier toward Anthony while Betty and Rosa were with us. Although they had never once asked why my business partner—as they viewed Anthony—and I lived together, shopped together, and arrived at parties together, they surely wondered. Now with my wife here, I fit into their social structure. Somehow they felt more at ease with us as a trio—husband, wife, and constant companion.

We showed Betty as much of Florianopolis and the island of Santa Catarina as possible. She also spent a day with us at Joaquim Beach watching us at work. Rosa, for her part, was so busy having fun with old friends that we hardly saw her other than at dinners and in passing.

All too soon it was over, and we found ourselves crowded into the kitchen, slicing and sautéing for a dinner together, just like back home at Anthony's condo, but with the addition of Rosa. Except this time it was a goodbye dinner. As I dished out the pasta and shrimp, and Anthony poured the wine, Betty started in with a torrent of thanks. "It's been like a dream," she said. "It may be old hat to all of you, but I've never been out of the United States before. I'm in awe of all this. I feel like a different person, and I can never, ever thank you enough."

"The person you should really thank is Ricardo," I said. "Give him our love and thank him from us, too." As the words left my mouth, I felt Anthony's stance stiffen. I hadn't told him about Ricardo buying Betty's ticket. He bristled whenever Ricardo's money played a role in anything, still, even after all this time.

"A big hug to Luigi," I told Rosa, "he earned it, taking care of the girls and the business this whole time."

"You know he's basking in it," Rosa said, "fully in charge of the girls and business without me telling him what to do."

Anthony tried to mask his stiffness as we drove Rosa and Betty to the airport, but once they boarded, the pleasantness was gone. He refused to speak to me for the entire ride back to Armacao. Then, when we were finally back home but not yet out of the car, he let loose. "How convenient—no mention of Ricardo's involvement until the trip was over. Not that anything would have gone differently if you had been honest from the start. My opinion means nothing to you. You refuse to face facts, to see your brother for what he is— a criminal."

I hated this, his steely anger. The assembly-line sentences, riveted together to form a wall of cold logic in front of him. It never failed to bring out the worst in me, as if maybe my tongue could turn into a blowtorch and the steel would fall away.

"How convenient that you managed to set your strong views aside when we used my criminal brother's money to found our business. Or wait, please refresh my memory, did you think those suitcases contained his earnings from the health club?"

"Don't bother with your sarcasm. We both know his request that you carry those suitcases wasn't a request at all, it was an order. You're just as much on his payroll as his bodyguards. And now you've allowed Betty to become indebted to him, too. How could you, after everything she has done for you? For us."

"You make him sound like the Godfather. *Credo*, Anthony, he may have some illegal dealings, but he's not a thug."

"How blind can you be? You seriously believe he hasn't hurt people, or paid someone else to do it for him?"

"I don't think about that! I don't want to. Whatever else he is, he's got a heart of gold. And he's my brother. Family. Have you forgotten what that means?"

I regretted it before the words left my mouth. Anthony's father had valued his career over his son, leaving a gash through the core of him. To turn family into a weapon in a fight, stabbing it into that unhealed wound, was the worst kind of betrayal.

Anthony flung open his door and stalked off into the blackness surrounding the car. I chased after him, kicking off my shoes so I could run across the sand without slipping. I reached out and grabbed the corner of his shirt, which had come untucked, and used it to pull him to me. He fought to get away, both of us struggling to gain purchase in the shifting sand. I felt him go still, then he crumpled into me. "I'm sorry, I'm sorry, I'm sorry," I said, over and over. The iron wall lay in pieces at our feet. "We're our own family, you and me."

"And Betty," he said, his voice thick.

"And Betty," I repeated. "Just us three."

CHAPTER NINETEEN

❧

A Divine Delivery

I closed my eyes sleepily and leaned back against the barraca. My mind drifted to the night before. Valentine's Day. I had cooked Anthony an aphrodisiac dinner: oysters, red grouper with a luxurious chili pepper sauce, and for dessert, honeyed figs with vanilla bean ice cream drizzled with dark chocolate sauce. After we enjoyed every last morsel, Anthony decided it would only be appropriate for him to show me his appreciation—and he had been very, very appreciative.

"Bruno?" I blinked back to reality, and found Marta standing before me. She seemed agitated, as if she were in a great hurry.

"Marta?" I said. "You look ready to burst out of your skin."

Anthony appeared from the other side of the barraca, where he had been tinkering with his caipirinha recipe.

"Padre Antonio sent me to ask you to come and see him. Now, he said."

Couldn't I have one day, just one, to bask in happiness?

"We'll come by as soon as we close the barraca," Anthony said.

Marta shifted from foot to foot. "Now would be better."

As committed as I was to helping the Padre counsel those dealing with HIV diagnoses, the last thing I wanted in that moment was to leave the sunbaked beach, to break the sweet morning-after mood. Great, I thought, this must be a really desperate case. I was being petty, but I resented relinquishing my afterglow.

When we entered Padre's living room, I was surprised to see that he was beaming from ear to ear. "My boys," he said delightedly. "Come, see, here, we have a gift." He led us into the bedroom. The shades were drawn against the midday sun. It was so dim I could barely make out the shapes of the furniture. Padre Antonio walked to the bed, and after pressing a finger to his lips to indicate we should stay quiet, he motioned to us to join him. As I drew nearer, I saw there were two small bundles lying on the center of the wide mattress. When I reached his side, I saw what the bundles were: babies. I had never seen such tiny humans before. I couldn't take my eyes off them. Both babies had rosy skin the color of lightly roasted coffee beans and dark, downy hair through which the tops of their miniature skulls were clearly visible.

"Now you understand why I wanted you to come right away," Padre Antonio said, "to meet these two. One is a boy and the other a girl, born to Maria this afternoon. The Maria I spoke to you about before. The one who buries her babies alive."

As I stood over those two fragile beings, Anthony at my side, the slight rasp of Padre's breath inside his chest, the utterly unthinkable cruelty of Maria's actions struck me full force.

"Finally, I found the strength to intervene," Padre continued. "And I have brought you and Anthony here because—after many prayers, the Holy Mother has directed me to give these infants to you, to raise as your own."

Anthony grabbed the crook of my elbow, and I wrapped my hand around his and squeezed.

"Maria may be crazy, but she's not stupid. She's deep in a drugged sleep right now, thanks to Isabela, the midwife who attended the delivery. But by evening, she's going to be awake. And if she sees any sign whatsoever of newborn twins near here, she will know that they are hers, no matter what we tell her. If you take the twins as yours, you'll have to leave immediately."

"But we can't just take them," Anthony said. "Two men travelling alone with two infants? We'll be arrested for kidnapping."

Padre Antonio nodded. "I thought of that. I have a doctor friend, and I'm close to a lawyer who attends my parish. I know that if I ask, they will prepare birth certificates and papers naming the mother as deceased and the father as Bruno—I think it would be best to name Bruno, as he is a native of Brazil."

"I don't know the first thing about babies," I said, more to myself than anyone else.

"I'm sure you'll get all the help you need from your family in Armacao, and wherever you go after that. I've gone over and over this in my head. Not only am I sure this would be the safest way to keep the twins alive—," here he paused and swallowed hard, "but I also know this to be God's will."

"I think we need a minute," I said.

"Not too long," said Padre Antonio, "Isabela says the drugs are strong, and that Maria should stay under for at least a few more hours, but how can we really know? Talk it over, but be quick. I will pray while I wait for your answer."

Despite the weight of the undertaking, Anthony and I were both convinced the twins had been sent to us for a reason. "Bruno, I've never let myself dream of becoming a father with you. Not once, not even for a second. It would have been too heartbreaking to entertain a possibility so amazing but so beyond the bounds of reality. Do you know what the odds are?

"I know," I said. "It was never even a question, was it, the idea that we—two gay men—could raise children together as our own? But still. I've never even changed a diaper. I'm scared shitless."

Anthony laughed. "Obviously, I am too. But at the same time, I'm 100 percent sure of what we need to do. You are too, right, Bruno?"

We returned to tell the Padre of our decision. Before we left, he baptized the babies. On the baptismal certificate, Anthony was named as the Godfather, and Betty as the Godmother in absentia.

We then did the only logical thing we could: headed home with our babies, our son and daughter. Ours! Overwhelming. The drive to my father's took longer than usual because I felt compelled to follow every driving rule I could remember. I left Anthony and the twins in the foyer with my utterly bewildered father. "I'll explain later, Dad, I promise," I'd called as I charged across the street to get Matilda.

"Come, come, come!" I said. "Matilda, I have to show you something! And I need your help."

Without pausing to untie her apron or ask a single question, Matilda ran back to my father's house with me. When she saw the twins, one cradled in Anthony's arms and the other held by my father, she looked stunned. "Whose—?"

"They're ours," I said. "Mine and Anthony's. I can't explain it all right now. The main thing is that Anthony and I have agreed to take these babies back to the United States and raise them as our own. So we need a crash course in parenthood. And some supplies. Will you come shopping with us?"

Matilda was literally beside herself. "Only if you tell me the rest of the story while we do that," she said, already kneeling down to investigate the bag Padre Antonio and Marta had sent with us. "It looks like you have enough formula and diapers for the night."

"OK, I trust you," I said. "So we'll shop tomorrow. Now, what about how we're holding them?"

Matilda looked at us long and hard, then burst out laughing. "You look fine, just terrified of those babies!" she said. "Terrified of them, but also in love with them. It's written all over your faces. And that's what really counts. The practical stuff I can teach you, but the bonding, that's God's work. It seems he did a good job here."

The next morning Matilda and I headed into Florianopolis. While she shopped for diapers and baby formula, I went to a law office to sign all the papers needed to prove my paternal rights—Padre's officially signed birth certificate was never once questioned—and within an hour I had the documents we would need to travel with the twins. I also bought airline tickets to get us to Rio. The flight departed in three days, and I planned to use every second of the time to absorb an encyclopedia of parenting know-how from Matilda.

Only after we spent the entire next day learning about bathing, feeding, diaper changing, swaddling, and so on, did any of us pause long enough to realize we had not yet given the babies names. We had simply been referring to them as the twins. Anthony knew immediately what he wanted to call our girl: "Roberta, after my mother." With that, our son's name was obvious: Rudolfo, after my father. I could see he was pleased and proud to have a namesake, but still mystified by the idea that Anthony and I would be raising two infants on our own.

Aside from the all-consuming task of learning how to care for Roberta and Rudulfo, whom we immediately nicknamed Rudi, we also had to find a way to pack or sell all our possessions. We would never have managed it on our own. My father took charge of selling our bus and our barraca equipment while Matilda hovered nearby to assist with our babies.

Anthony and I both found many aspects of childcare to be surprisingly instinctive. Others, however, were inordinately baffling. The umbilical cords proved particularly puzzling. Had Matilda not been there to enlighten us, neither of us would have known the little nubs would eventually dry and fall off, nor that we should avoid immersing the babies in water until the cords were completely healed. These blind spots kept me up at night, tossing and turning over the enormity of what we had pledged to do, and the terrifying prospect of screwing it up. Was this what it felt like to be a father?

On February 19, 1997, after a last series of goodbyes (stoic on my father's part, teary on Matilda's), we flew from Florianopolis to Rio. I had called Paulo to ask if we could come and stay for a while. When we finally arrived at Paulo and Dina's after an easy flight—lucky for us the babies slept the entire way, including as we navigated the airport—the sun had dropped below the Rio skyline. I hadn't known how to explain our two new additions over the phone, and decided to do it in person.

Dina answered the door with a sauce-covered spoon in her hand. When she saw the babies, who were still sleepy and calm in our arms, she dropped the spoon and gasped. Paulo came running, but the worry on his face shifted into a smitten grin as soon as he spotted the twins. "Looks like you have news," he said. Anthony and I took turns explaining every detail of how we came to have Roberta and Rudi in our care.

Dina volunteered to stay home the following day and help Anthony care for the babies while I dealt with the U.S. Consulate's office. Again, the birth certificates and papers that Padre Antonio had bestowed upon us were all in perfect order. Not a single question was raised.

Five days later, we boarded our flight to Miami. Before we left, I called Rosa and Betty to tell them to expect us at 8 a.m., and that there would be two more passengers with us. I wanted to see their faces when they learned the news—or better yet, got to hold the news in their arms. Once again, Roberta and Rudi slept through the flight, but this time they grew restless and started to cry when the wheels hit the tarmac. Their dislike of the landing process had a hidden benefit—thanks to sympathetic officials, we made it off the airplane, through immigration, and past customs in thirty minutes flat. When we stepped onto U.S. soil, well, technically, tile, both Rosa and Betty were there waiting to welcome us back. Their expressions when they saw Anthony and me, each of us with a babe in arms, were priceless: a combination of complete disbelief and utter joy. Rosa actually burst into tears and didn't stop crying until we'd reached the car. We all agreed to go to Betty's house so we could tell our story.

It took nearly an hour to wend our way through Miami's rush-hour traffic to Betty's little bungalow. Poor Roberta and Rudi, overwhelmed by the influx of unfamiliar sights, sounds, and smells, cried almost the entire way there. "You make the formula," I told Anthony as we parked in front of Betty's, "and I'll do the diaper changing."

"Listen to you two," Betty said. "Already experts."

"For sure," I said. "We've got it down."

When both of our tiny international travelers were bathed, dressed in fresh clothes, and sleeping soundly, we adults could finally talk. In breathless torrents of words, Anthony and I spilled out the story, both talking over each other in our excitement to cover every detail.

When we finished, a few moments elapsed before Betty or Rosa spoke.

"So," Betty said, "this priest just ... stole them?"

"No, he saved them," Anthony said. "From being killed by their mother."

Both women looked—I couldn't tell what it was, exactly. Dubious? Worried? Both, maybe.

"You realize that were it not for Padre Antonio—and I suppose to a lesser degree, for Anthony and me—these babies would be either dead or abandoned," I said. "I can't understand why you seem so disapproving."

"Don't get defensive," Rosa said. "I believe the padre did a heroic thing. It's just that, this is, it's a huge commitment. It would be one thing to take care of them for a period of time. But how are you guys going to do this forever? Do you really think you're equipped to be parents?"

Anthony and I tried to remain unruffled, but after all we had already been through, we felt strongly bonded to our newly formed family. We made it clear that any assistance either woman had to offer would be welcome, but blood ties be damned, Roberta and Rudi were our children. Nothing could change that.

Betty had the condo cleaned and ready for our arrival—the tenants had moved out on the first of the month—but she hadn't known we would be taking care of babies. So she dropped Anthony, Roberta and Rudi, and the suitcases at the condo, then she and I went shopping for cribs.

"We need a car," I told Anthony that first night, after we finally got the babies to sleep. "A practical one." By the end of the next day, Anthony had traded his beloved Corvette for a four-door Tahoe.

"But now we need a pediatrician!" he said as we lay exhausted on the couch that night. "Rosa must have one. You have to ask her." Every day it was the same: we cleared one hurdle, spotted another, got a running start and jumped again, then found ourselves back at the starting line. I guess you could say we were settling into the rhythm of parenthood.

CHAPTER TWENTY

Growing Pains

Apart from the seismic perspective shift brought about by the fact that we were now parents, our life in Miami was much the same as it had been. I went back to work at the health club and in just two weeks, not only were my classes full, but I also had waiting lists once again. I was having so much fun I felt almost guilty, like I should have been the one paying for the classes. Anthony was happy to take charge of Roberta and Rudi while I taught. If he ever felt overwhelmed, both Rosa and Betty were at the ready to tag in. So ready, in fact, that they were constantly bickering over whose turn it was. That tension didn't make the tough days of raising two infants any easier, but both Anthony and I agreed it was better to have two willing (if combative) babysitters on call than to have none, so we did what we could to ensure they both felt we were divvying up auxiliary childcare fairly.

As time passed, Rosa's attention naturally gravitated back to her own children. Marlene was getting ready to start kindergarten, and

Rosa was beside herself over her babies growing up. I had to admit, Marlene did look huge next to Roberta and Rudi. Betty, on the other hand, continued to check in almost daily. Would we have made it through that first year without her? I can't see how. More than a babysitter, more than an aunt, she became something closer to a third parent—and an extremely controlling one at that.

Betty had firm ideas about how things should be done when it came to our twins, but in the end, her bossy and invasive ways were a small price to pay for her help. The language to describe our unconventional arrangement was lacking, but that didn't matter because clearly, it worked. In some of our rare moments to ourselves, when both twins were quietly sleeping and we had yet to slide into unconsciousness, Anthony and I wondered whether we were holding Betty back from some other, more conventional life.

"She picked me," I would remind us both.

"But she couldn't have foreseen this," Anthony would say. "It's not normal."

"No one could have foreseen this. The point is, I don't think she wants normal."

Meanwhile Anna and Jim—even though they had not yet met the twins— embraced our new family members from afar. It seemed a package from Minnesota showed up every week. Somehow, Anna seemed to track the rapidly growing twins' clothing sizes more accurately than I did.

There were, naturally, days Anthony accused me of turning him into a hausfrau. "I'm covered in spit-up, you could pack the entirety of Gucci's spring collection in the bags under my eyes, and you're prancing off to aerobics where you get to stare at tight asses in spandex."

"At least your wittiness remains intact?"

He threw a burp cloth at me, and burst into tears.

"Hey, hey," I said, drawing him into my arms, ignoring the smell of the spit-up. "First of all, most of the asses in my classes belong to women over forty hoping to drop a few pounds. Second of all, I can handle more of the night feedings—you're exhausted, I can see that. I'm not trying to shirk my responsibilities, I'm just a heavy sleeper. You might have to wake me up. Punch me if you need to, OK?"

Even in his blackest moods, Anthony's patience with the twins never faltered. He read to them for hours on end, little heads snuggled up against him on both sides, and the book propped against his legs. The three of them were regulars at the local library's story hour. They hauled stacks of books home after every visit. Considering the sheer volume of words they heard each day, it's no wonder both of our twins were early talkers.

Roberta's first word was ball, quickly followed by Papa—always directed at Anthony, never at me. I may have been the one listed on their birth certificates, but he was the one who cared for them, day in and day out. We settled on Dada for me, which switched to Dad as they grew older. Betty's nickname came straight from Rudi. He spontaneously greeted her when she appeared at the door one day as Beebee! It's hard to say whose smile was bigger: Rudi's, at the joy of having successfully communicated a new word, or Beebee's, at the undeniable indication of her importance to the twins.

As I danced around the kitchen one February day in 2001, still marveling that this new year had also rung in a new millennium, and updating my moves in recognition of that—I was struck by a brilliant idea. The twins were almost four, and the condo was seeming more and more cramped. They needed sunshine and fresh air, and I had a scheme to make it happen for them. Our apartment was on the fourth floor, the top floor of the building. Directly adjacent to our kitchen was a deck. Why not landscape the area with planters full of trees and flowers? If I constructed a wall, the twins could play there with no danger whatsoever of falling. The plan worked out wonderfully, and to Rudi and Roberta's delight, I included a bright plastic pool.

Anthony was stunned when he saw my handiwork. "Yet another talent, urban landscaping," he said. "It's beautiful—and so logical. It looks like it should always have been here, like an extension of the apartment. Our own garden." The twins loved to play on the deck, and Anthony and I loved to relax and watch them splash in the shallow, warm water of their kiddie pool.

For the twins' fourth birthdays, to Anthony's and my delight and surprise, Rosa and Betty collaborated to throw a truly massive party in Betty's backyard. "They're old enough to enjoy a birthday party now," Betty said, "and it needs to be a miracle party, for our miracle babies." Both Roberta and Rudulfo were quite clear on what a birthday was all about, and their expectations were sky high. Still, the special festivities planned by Beebee and Tia Rosa completely awed them—and us.

Our neighborhood comprised mostly young families, all of who seemed to show up for the big day. Marlene and Bridgette were there with bells on, of course. Ricardo was away managing an unspecified situation, but Beth came with Marco. Every time I saw him, he looked more and more like my brother. He fit right in with his cousins and the neighbor kids who whooped and ran endlessly around the yard.

By the time dusk descended, both Roberta and Rudi were

sound asleep on Betty's couch, their shiny, plastic birthday crowns askew. As we collected the wrapping paper strewn about the living room, I filled Betty and Rosa in on the plan Anthony and I had recently hatched. "We need to spend some time in Minnesota," I explained. "I want the twins to meet my American parents. Anna and Jim have been so patient, but they're dying for us to come. And since we really want the twins to experience snow, we're leaving next week."

"Bruno," Betty said, "you should know that it's not that unusual for there to be snow in May."

Betty, Betty, always the know-it-all. I threw a handful of paper curlicues at her. "Well, I'm not taking any chances. We want to give them the perfect winter getaway."

We arrived in Minneapolis during the last week of February. Anna and Jim assured us we were welcome to stay as long as we liked, so we planned to stay a full two weeks. Anna had set up a spare bedroom like a nursery, brimming over with even more presents. Not to be outdone, Jim took the role of honorary grandpa with gusto, telling elaborate stories about his childhood in Minnesota—which our warm-weather babies viewed as a highly exotic land.

Both Roberta and Rudi loved to play in the sparkling, cold whiteness of the snow. Anna and Jim gamely took them sledding whenever they wished, much to Anthony's and my relief. Neither of us was quite as charmed by winter as our children were. I must admit, though, that watching the pure delight and exhilaration that lit their faces as they sped down the powdery slopes did more to keep me warm than my horrible, puffy down coat. Maybe we overdid all the outdoor play, because by the second week—in spite of their layers and layers of snowsuits, hats, mittens, and scarves—Roberta and Rudi both had bad colds. It was just like Anna had always said about my siblings and me: the twins just weren't used to the weather, their immune systems weren't calibrated to protect them.

On Saturday morning, as the coughing and sneezing became near constant, we all agreed it would be best to lie low for a day. So I seized the opportunity to visit some old friends in St. Paul, while Anthony stayed at Anna's and Jim's. "Are you sure?" I asked Anthony after Jim offered to let me use his car. "I don't want to leave you on your own. Would you rather I stayed, too?"

"You're sweet to ask, but it's more than OK for you to take off," Anthony insisted. "I feel a little tickle in the back of my own throat this morning, so a couch day is exactly what I need. Have fun in St. Paul. We'll see you for dinner?"

"Definitely." I kissed him and everyone else goodbye and headed out.

When I returned after a long, delightful afternoon of catching up, I found the house dark and empty. A hastily scrawled note on the kitchen table awaited me: "Drive to Children's Hospital ASAP!!!" Without bothering to put my coat back on, I sprinted to Jim's Honda.

I have no memory of the drive to the hospital. When I ran into the waiting room, I saw Anthony, Anna, Jim, and Rudi huddled together by the courtesy phone. Anna spotted me first and nudged Anthony, who was clutching the receiver with one hand and holding Rudi close to his chest with the other. As soon as Anthony saw me, his fragile composure cracked and he began to sob. Anna gently scooped Rudi into her own arms as I wrapped Anthony in mine.

Through his tears, Anthony conveyed the key facts: he heard a rattle in Roberta's chest, and when he took her temperature, it registered at 104 degrees. Anna drove as fast as the icy roads would allow, with Anthony in the front seat holding Roberta and Jim in the back trying to keep Rudi calm. At the hospital, a doctor diagnosed Roberta with advanced pneumonia and immediately sent her to intensive care. Only immediate family members were allowed in the unit, the doctor explained. Neither Anna, Jim, nor Anthony was a blood relation or legal guardian, so the hospital refused to allow them in with Roberta.

"What kind of fucked-up bullshit . . . ." I said. "I won't stand for it." I approached the nurses' station and identified myself as Roberta's father. "I want to see her immediately," I said. "And he'll be coming back with me." I pointed over to Anthony. The nurses agreed to take me back to the ICU, but they adamantly refused to admit Anthony.

"Just go!" he said. "She's alone back there! Just go, Bruno."

Roberta was sleeping by the time I reached her side. A sort of plastic tent contraption covered her bed. "It makes it easier for her to breathe," the nurses explained. I had barely heard a word of the doctor's explanation. All I knew was that her dark curls were terribly matted, and I could not lift the plastic to smooth them. I fought back tears as I sat and listened to the rough whistle of her breath.

After three days of antibiotics and oxygen therapy, Roberta's fever finally broke. Her breathing had improved as well. "Where's Papa?" she asked. Anthony was her definite favorite, and it crushed me to see her senselessly separated from him when she needed him most. He'd have been right here beside her if only the hospital would allow it. As Roberta continued to improve over the course of that fourth day, her doctor agreed to move her to a semi-private room. Finally, Anthony could see our baby girl. Her smile when he walked into the room filled up her whole face. I surprised them both by bursting into tears—partially from relief, and partially from fury that he had been kept away for so long.

CHAPTER TWENTY-ONE

Better or For Worse

We had been back in Miami for close to a month, and the excitement and stress of our Minnesota trip was well behind us. Yet Anthony still seemed off-kilter. One night, when he yet again turned off the light and slid into bed without saying a word, I finally came out and asked what was eating at him.

"Nothing, really," he said.

"Don't give me that. You've been upset about something ever since we left Minnesota."

He sighed. "I don't have any answers, Bruno. Not for this, right here, right now, or for the future."

"What in the world are you talking about?"

"I can't stop replaying what happened at the hospital. I go over and over it in my mind. Do you realize, Bruno, that I have no rights to our babies? I'm not their father. I'm not a legal guardian. I'm not anything."

"Not anything? You know that's a lie." I crept over to his side of the bed and pressed my face into the back of his neck. "Fuck the hospital," I whispered. "You are their father and you always will be, to me and to them. That's what counts."

He rolled over to face me. "Wouldn't it be nice if that were true. But it's not, Bruno. It's just not. It doesn't hold up. If anything happened to you, I would lose them. Permanently. I dream about that—accidents, illnesses, hospitals—me stuck in the waiting room, hammering at the glass door while the nurses laugh and laugh." His voice creaked. "We've been together for more than six years. We've lived together longer than you and Betty ever did, but if you lay there dying, who would be allowed to sit by your side?"

"I'm so sorry, *querido*. I don't have answers either. I can't change the laws, and I can't promise that I, or Rudi, or Roberta, won't ever get sick. All I can say is that right now, we're all fine. We're all here. We all love you. If anything, the kids love you more than me!" I laughed, but Anthony kept his face locked. "Just try to focus on the present moment, the here and now," I said.

He held my palm to his cheek. "I'll try," he said. "God knows, I have been."

Months passed, and Anthony's mood lingered. Whenever it felt a breaking point was looming, after which I would have to take some dire steps like forcing him into therapy or taking the twins to stay with Betty for a while, a good day would appear.

It was during this same time that he invented Grin, a friendly but misunderstood tiger. Poor Grin just wanted to make friends, but his scary tiger smile made all the other animals run away. Anthony would flash his teeth and chase the twins around the apartment as they shrieked and giggled. When they all ran out of breath, he would gather Rudi and Roberta into his arms and tell long, intricate stories about Grin's world. It was a place filled with exotic tiger foods, magical plants that didn't grow anywhere else, and an especially nasty female tiger named Snark who tormented Grin relentlessly.

Too much of the time, though, Anthony seemed depressed, distant, or angry. And it wasn't just his mood that was tanking. There were physical changes, too. His running habit dwindled. He barely ate. I was scared. How could I not be? But he brushed off any questions about his health with pat answers about not enough sleep and too many responsibilities, the kind of martyr crap that he'd never have put up with from me in a million years. Anthony had always been the one who monitored both our conditions so carefully, the one who scheduled our regular check-ups, who tracked news coverage about clinical trials. And yet now all I heard was, "Parenting tires everyone out. How many stay-at-home moms do you know who go for regular runs?" His laugh was dry and joyless.

I had grown accustomed to falling asleep to accounts of his days with Roberta and Rudi. Even the hard days sounded wonderful in his retellings. The tantrums were always resolved, the tears and snot were rinsed off, the sore spot left when a childish hand gave a hard yank to a hunk of hair was gently rubbed until it felt better. Now I was lucky if I got a sentence or two. Pressed for more, he'd sigh and say, "I'm all worn out, Bruno," then lapse into silence.

"You let them watch too much TV," he snapped one evening. "Technicolor idiocy. You're melting their brains."

"Everyone loves the *Teletubbies*," I protested. "How can you not? Unless you're Jerry Falwell. And I'm tired—."

"You're tired? After dancing around all day? I bet that was just exhausting."

I tried to rub his shoulders. He shrugged my hands away impatiently, but not before I felt how unexpectedly bony they were. How long had it been since I had really touched his body?

"Why don't we take a night for ourselves?" I suggested. "I'll call Betty now—you know she'd be thrilled to have the twins sleep over, and they love staying at her house."

"Don't bother," Anthony replied. "I'm going to bed."

He stooped slowly to kiss Roberta's and Rudi's cheeks, then walked into our bedroom and shut the door.

November arrived, bringing sunlight that was rich but with so little heat. One evening when I returned from work, Anthony met me at the door.

"I'm flying to Venezuela," he said. "I leave tomorrow. My sister Daniela got my number somehow—my father passed away. A massive heart attack. My mother is asking for me."

I pulled him into my arms. I wanted to say, "I'm going with you," but I hesitated. So we stood there, wordless. I could feel his heartbeat against my chest, fragile, human. I loved him so intensely. "Of course you have to go," I said. "Your mother is asking for you, Anthony! Don't worry about us. Stay as long as you need."

The next twenty-four hours were a mad, sad dash of packing and planning. Rosa came to the condo to watch the twins while Betty and I drove Anthony to the airport. I managed to stay calm until his plane soared off into the stark sky. Then I crumpled. I spent the night clutching his pillow to my chest, drifting in and out of worried wakefulness and dreams about some menace I needed to warn my family about, except that I had lost the ability to speak. Every time I thought I was done crying, something set me off again.

By the end of the first week, I couldn't stand it anymore. If Daniela could find our number, I could find hers. When I finally did, it took me another day to gather my nerve to dial it. But I needn't have worried. The other end of the line just rang and rang, not even an answering machine. I hung up and redialed, to the same effect. I called the number so many times that I learned it by heart, the crumpled paper I'd written it on now discarded.

Two weeks went by this way, with no contact. Betty supplied a stream of possible reasons to explain Anthony's silence: the time difference, funeral arrangements, reconciling (or fighting) with his family. She essentially moved into the condo and did everything she could to distract the twins and me.

Then, finally, a call came. "I'm glad I'm here," he told me, his voice soft and shaky. "My family needs me. I think I . . . ." He paused. "I think I'm going to stay here over the holidays. I'm not sure—." Again, he trailed off.

I wanted to scream into the phone, I wanted to tell him to go to hell and get on a plane at the same time. But a cold emptiness, a kind of fear I couldn't name, wound itself around my tongue and stopped me. "If you think that's best," I said. "I understand. I do. When do you think . . . ."

"Bruno, I don't know. I can't say right now."

Christmas came and went, and then New Year's. I tried to be patient. I tried not to push. I reminded myself that it had been years since he had been home, or even spoken to his family. He had grieved over the fact he might never do either of those things again. Of course he wanted to stay. Of course he was preoccupied.

When Anthony called, which never happened more than once in the same week, he said very little—almost nothing, in fact. If I brought up the topic of his return, he hemmed and hawed. "Put Roberta back on. I miss my girl," he'd say.

The twins missed him fiercely, and clung to me with an unprecedented ferociousness in his absence. We three clung to each other, I suppose. I rearranged my schedule to minimize the blocks of time they spent without me. As their fifth birthday drew near, I grew firmer in my demands that Anthony at least set a date for his return. He dodged every request. "It's complicated," he said.

"Complicated how? I don't understand. I'm not going to chain you up if you come home. You could always go back if you need to. Maybe bring me and the twins with you," I said.

His calls became more and more infrequent.

Betty counseled patience, even when I turned on her. "Does he call you? I know he does. Don't deny it. What has he told you?"

"Bruno, I don't know any more than you do. If I did know anything, how could you believe I would keep it from you, from Roberta, from Rudi?"

"I know. I'm sorry. It's just so fucking hard."

She took my face into her hands and cradled it.

Spring came, and I began to adjust to the new status quo. I still missed him, achingly, like I had broken a bone that was knitting back together all wrong. Between my classes, Roberta and Rudi, grocery shopping, car payments, and Rosa's continual urges to renovate or upgrade some facet of the club, I didn't have the time to harangue my absentee lover about his whereabouts. I knew if I let myself dwell on Anthony's disappearance, I would be consumed by it.

In June, he finally told me what I had been waiting to here. "I'm flying back to Miami," he said.

"*Graças a Deus!*"

"Bruno, listen. It will only be a short visit. One week."

I was stunned. The anger I had refused to acknowledge for the past months surfaced all at once. "One week? For a visit? Is this your idea of a joke? You know what, don't even bother."

"Bruno, I can't talk for long—."

"Of course you can't, you miserable *crápula*—."

"I know this can't have been easy on you," he cut in. "My going away. I'm surprised you didn't lose your temper with me sooner. I know you've wanted to, you've had the right to. But the fact remains that I have to come back, and I want to see you when I do. And my babies, but—." His voice caught in his throat. "Maybe that would be selfish. I don't want to scare them. Bruno. I don't want to scare you. I'm in a wheelchair now. I can't walk. I can't do a lot of things. I don't want to burden you any more than I have to, and I'll need 24-hour care while I'm there, so I'm bringing a nurse."

I couldn't talk. I couldn't breathe.

"An accident?"

"No. An infection. In my brain."

The world spun. My legs gave out. I dropped the phone and landed hard on my knees, sobs pouring out of me.

"Please, Bruno. Bruno, my love." His voice, tinny and weak, was just audible from the phone lying on its side on the floor. I picked it back up and held it to my ear again. "Now can you see why I stayed away?" he was saying.

"Not fair."

"None of this is fair," he said with a sharp, hysterical sounding laugh. "The reason I'm flying home is to say goodbye. The doctors think I'm an idiot for trying to travel, but, well. It's called progressive multifocal leukoencephalopathy. PML. A complication of AIDS. Fatal, Bruno. There is no treatment. But they're doing their best to make me comfortable. It's in my brain. I said that, right? I get foggy, and I can't quite speak all the time. I meant it when I said I can't talk for long. I never know when the words will stop coming out right. Anyway. I have to come back now, while I'm still coherent, so I can turn over ownership of the condo to the twins, with you as their guardian."

The cries just kept coming out of me. I couldn't stop and I couldn't catch my breath.

"Try to listen, Bruno. Please. I want you to talk to Rosa. Have her prepare all of the legal documents before I arrive so I won't have to deal with it, and we can spend as much time together as possible. Can you do that for me?"

I went alone to meet his flight. Seeing him knocked the wind out of me. He had lost over fifty pounds. His clothes hung on him, accentuating bones that had previously been wrapped in layers of well-toned muscle. He managed a wan smile when he saw me. I took his hands in mine and knelt by his chair.

"Not now," he said. "Not here. Can't you see the stares?"

I had promised myself I wouldn't make a scene.

"This is Alberto," he said, gesturing behind him to the man pushing his chair. I rose to my feet and shook Alberto's hand.

"The twins?" he asked.

"They're sleeping."

"Right, right, it's late here."

As soon as we reached the condo, Anthony insisted on seeing

Roberta and Rudi. With effort, he pulled himself out of the chair. Alberto rushed to offer him an arm to lean on, but he waved him away. Without a word, I wrapped my arm around his waist. He was so slight, as if a hard squeeze might break him. He let me help him into the twins' room. Both were sleeping soundly. Grasping my shoulder tightly, he leaned to give them each a kiss on the cheek. I could see that he, too, was ready to sleep. I offered to sleep on the couch and let him have the bed. I wasn't sure what the boundaries were. I had been thinking it over since he called. "I bought a cot," I said, "for your nurse. For Alberto. I got pillows and blankets too, so he should be comfortable."

"Thank you," Anthony said simply.

The next morning I woke early and prepared a large breakfast: homemade sweet rolls, vegetable frittata, papaya juice and espresso, all his favorites. As soon as Anthony awoke, the twins rushed in to see him. They were unfazed by his bony frame, and more curious than disturbed by the chair. "Can we push you?" Rudi wanted to know. I ducked into the bedroom to hide the tears. Always the damn tears.

Though the twins seemed untroubled by the chair, Anthony hated for them to see him in it. "I don't want them to remember me like this," he said. "Or you," he added.

"We just want to be close to you. I want to be close to you. For better or worse, even if you never made an honest woman of me."

That, finally, got a laugh out of him.

"I missed your jokes."

"I would have flown to you, you know. If you had told me. I would have found a way to be there with you. I would have told you all the jokes."

"I know. But. I didn't want, things had been rough. And maybe, if I just stayed away, I thought—."

"You idiot."

We slept in the same bed that night, Anthony's head snug against my shoulder. Alberto moved his cot to the living room where he was still close at hand should he be needed. The relief of holding him again, waking up to his face each morning, listening as he read to Roberta and Rudi just like the old days, was marred by the knowledge of how temporary the reunion would be. He refused to discuss the possibility of us all returning to Venezuela together. "My family," he said. "It's just not possible. They would never understand, Bruno."

Soon, much too soon, the day of his departure arrived. For the twins' sake, I tried to hold back my tears. Betty, Rosa, Luigi, their kids, and even Ricardo went to the airport to send Anthony off with love. Putting aside his usual machismo, and with complete disregard for the social stigma surrounding men in the last, all-too-visible stages of AIDS, Ricardo bent over Anthony's wheelchair and kissed him on both cheeks. "You are my brother," he said, "just as much as Bruno is. And your children are my family, too. They will never want for anything. I promise you."

"Thank you," Anthony said.

He looked at me with so much softness, so much love, so much regret. My heart was breaking. He'll come back, I told myself. I'll see him again.

Nine days later, I received a call from Alberto. "He gave me a note with this number on it," Alberto said. "I promised him I would call. He wanted you to know he wasn't in any pain at the end . . . .."

I don't remember a single word after that, only going to the high cupboard where we kept the *cachaça*, a souvenir of our happy time in Brazil. Anthony wanted to bring some back so we could serve caipirinhas when we entertained. Sometime not long after I opened that bottle, the room went black and the next thing I remember was waking up with Betty standing over me.

Apparently I had the presence of mind to call her before I'd downed all the liquor, although I doubt I got any real words out. "When I found you," Betty told me later, "you said you were going to keep drinking until your brain shut off." She promptly moved the twins and me into her house until I got through the initial shock.

When I was able to think about his death without wanting to die myself, the irony struck me. Anthony—who had insisted that I take care of myself, who was so convinced we could live long, long lives—was the first of us to die. Some days, I felt sure his death meant God had turned away from me, that it was a sign telling me to let the worst parts of myself run roughshod over the rest of me. Why try so hard to be good, for nothing? Some days I cursed the members of his family who were still living for stealing his last days from me. Some days I cursed myself for not going with him, not grabbing hold when he pulled away. Other days, I acknowledged in the end, his family accepted and loved him as best they could. Other days, I felt the only way I had left to show my love for him was to continue to live the life he had compelled me to want for myself. I tried to hang on to that.

Anthony never could accept things as they were; instead, he saw the best possible way something could be. The real cause of his death, I am convinced, was double heartbreak. He was still recovering from the trauma of being separated from Roberta at the hospital in Minneapolis when his father died before they had the chance to reconcile. Anthony set his own terms, and made the world live up to them. He refused to stop striving to bring his life in line with his vision of what could be, even if it killed him. It did.

CHAPTER TWENTY-TWO

Roots

The only thing harder than hearing the news of Anthony's death myself was trying to help the twins understand. Roberta, especially, was devastated. He had always been her clear favorite—and no wonder. He treated her like an absolute princess. Even more than that, they were linked by the ways she was just like him: her sensitivity, idealism, and kindness. Now it was up to me to show our children that everything would be all right without him. The problem was that I was struggling to believe it myself.

The calendar doesn't care about heartbreak. Before we three knew what hit us, school was back in session. Then, just as we were settling back into some semblance of a routine, Halloween arrived to kick off the holiday season. Thanksgiving, Christmas, and New Year's followed in quick succession. Betty and Rosa worked overtime to keep everyone busy. That thing they say about keeping busy to stave back grief? It's true. As we marched from one event to the next, as we marked off each holiday with an extravaganza even bigger than the last, I eventually began to sleep and wake without crying.

Suddenly it was February 15, 2003, and Betty was lighting twelve birthday candles—six on each cake. They were growing up so fast, too fast. When school let out in June, I announced my plan. "I'm taking the twins to Brazil," I told Betty. "Roberta and Rudi are Brazilian, and I want them to learn to speak their language correctly. Even more importantly, I want them to be able to read and write in Portuguese. We'll leave next month, I think, and stay a whole year."

Betty looked unsurprised. "You worry about packing anything you think you'll need," she said, "and I'll take care of everything here." She meant what she said, too. She found renters for the apartment, a space to store the car until we returned, and flat-out made the process of arranging an international trip with two six-year-olds seem entirely manageable.

We flew directly from Miami to Brasilia. My father was waiting for us at the airport, which I expected. What I didn't expect was how he looked: emaciated and skeletal, just like Anthony on his final trip to Miami. My father was seventy years old, but he appeared much, much older. He seemed shrunken. His energy and zest were gone. I soon learned why. His lifestyle had finally caught up with him. He had inoperable lung cancer.

I called Rosa and Ricardo as soon as I could that evening. Ricardo wasted no time. He had just purchased a new airplane, "State of the art—the 2003 Sierra Eagle II/501SP." It was, he informed me in his usual way, more than capable of making the trip in record time and incomparable comfort. After coordinating with Rosa, he relayed that they would be taking off from Kissimmee St. Cloud before dawn the next morning. With two refueling stops, one at the Fernando Juiz Ribas Dominican Republic airport and the other at the Boa Vista Atlas Basil Catanhede Airport, Ricardo estimated the flight would take just under twelve hours.

Late the following afternoon, I asked my father if he'd like to take a drive with me. I didn't give a reason, and he didn't ask. He rarely left his bed except to see the doctor, so even a purposeless car ride was a welcome diversion. We arrived at the airport in time to see an elegant private plane descend onto a side runway. As we pulled in closer, my father realized the waving figures walking out of the plane and down the steps were Rosa and Ricardo. Stoic as he typically was, he couldn't hold back his tears. The glance we siblings shared between us conveyed a shared sentiment: the whole trip was already well worth it.

Once he wiped his eyes, my father wanted to know every detail about the purchase of the plane and the flight over. "*Filho*, do you have any idea what this will cost you?" As always, both my father and my sister were ceaselessly impressed by Ricardo's wealth, and equally unburdened by thoughts about how he attained it, and at what cost to others. I couldn't help but think of Anthony, who insisted I take a long look at the moral quicksand my brother was stuck in. But certainly now was not the time for me to wrestle with Ricardo's wrongdoings. I reminded myself of Ricardo's kindnesses to Betty while Anthony and I were in Florianopolis. Even more striking was the image of his tenderness with Anthony on that heartbreaking last visit before his death, his declaration that Anthony was family, and that the twins would never want for anything, and the genuine gratitude and remorse in Anthony's eyes.

"Of course I know what it will cost," Ricardo answered. "My budget was just under $20,000 each way. Based on this leg, I'd say I was close, the fuel should cost close to $39,000 round trip." Though the airplane could be flown by a single pilot, Ricardo had brought his assistant, John, who also had his private pilot certification and instrument rating. Ricardo wanted someone to stay on the plane because he would not take the chance of leaving such a prized aircraft unattended.

We all knew this would be the last time we would be together, and were determined to make the most of every minute. Rosa spent the two days glued to our father's side, telling stories, reminiscing, and letting him know how much he was loved. Ricardo stayed close too, only leaving the house once to collect a package delivered to him directly from Rio de Janeiro. Rosa and I both knew better than to ask for specifics. Each for our own reasons, we both felt that the less we knew about Ricardo's business dealings, the better.

Just days after Rosa and Ricardo left, our father took a turn for the worse. The pain caused by breathing became excruciating. He was admitted to the hospital where his medications and oxygen could be more readily monitored. Despite the pain and heavy medication, he gripped tightly to consciousness.

When I took the twins to see him on September 7, he haltingly explained the tradition of Brazilian Independence Day. "Prince Pedro, who was next in line to be king of Portugal, fell in love with Brazil, he said in a slow, weak voice. "When Portugal demanded loyalty to him, as their king, he gave us our independence then and there. On September 7, 1822, Prince Pedro proclaimed that Brazil was truly independent and no longer a colony of Portugal.

Remember that date, always celebrate it, and think of your old grandpa." I think it was his determination not to spoil the holiday for his grandchildren that kept him alive until 12:07 a.m. on September 8.

In Brazil there is no embalming, so we buried my father the next day. It seemed like the whole town of Brasilia came to pay their honors. After the funeral, I delivered reports over the phone to Rosa and Ricardo, then Betty, and then to Anna and Jim. "The saddest thing," I told them, "is that he missed his own funeral. He would have loved to be there, celebrating, telling stories of his youth, singing, dancing, and carrying on."

After I settled my father's affairs, I took the twins to Florianopolis. Matilda met us at the airport and took us to my father's house in Armacao Beach. The twins loved it all so much! The house was only one block from the beach and had a swimming pool as well, thanks to my father's projects during that last year I spent in Armacao with Anthony. Perhaps their favorite element, however was that the house was on a dead-end street lined with kids. They gathered in hordes to play game after game on that street without so much as a single worry about intrusive cars. Right away, Roberta and Rudi fell in love with soccer. They played for hours. Sometimes—when enough motivated kids got involved—they trekked to the soccer field a quarter of a kilometer away.

After the twins settled into a rhythm in Florianopolis, I took them to see Padre Antonio who, miracle of miracles, was still alive—but barely. Right after he entrusted the twins to Anthony and me, he suffered a major stroke that left him paralyzed and in a wheel chair. He'd been living in a care facility run by the Sisters of Charity. "He had another stroke two months before you got here,"

Matilda had told me. "It affected his speech this time. The doctors don't think he has long."

Roberta and Rudi had grown up on stories of Padre Antonio, the hero who saved their lives and who chose Anthony and me to be their dads based on God's direction. When the day came to meet him, they were beside themselves with nerves. For me, seeing him wheelchair-bound and unable to speak was bittersweet. I could see from his expression that he recognized me when I walked in. I cleared my throat and swallowed back the tears. "Padre," I said, "these are the babies, the babies you gave to Anthony and me. You could have lit the room with his smile. He lifted his arms. After quick glances up at me to get the go-ahead, the twins ran over to him, kissed his wrinkled cheeks, and settled down beside his wheelchair.

I knew he would want to know where Anthony was, even though he couldn't ask. The question was bright in his eyes. So I told him the truth. He looked so sad, and so tired. After only a few minutes in his company, the sister who had announced our arrival returned to usher us away. I heard from Matilda that just two days later, he peacefully passed away and went to his reward.

Matilda, who tracked every event (minor and major) that took place in her community, also related news of Maria, the twins' birth mother. The report was both happy and sad. Happily, she had no more children and therefore made no more sacrifices to the Rainha de Mar. Sadly, but all too predictably, she contracted HIV and died two years after we left Brazil.

We stayed in Florianopolis until the end of February. School would begin in March, and I wanted to enroll Roberta and Rudi in Brasilia, where the weather didn't get as cold as it did by the sea. I also believed they would receive a better education in the capital city than anywhere else in Brazil. The way they adjusted amazed me. It was as if they'd been going to Brazilian school their whole lives. Between their love of soccer and their natural openness, they were soon surrounded with friends. Once they finished their homework in the afternoons, they sped off to the local soccer field where they played until dark.

The months rolled along, and I began planning our departure. Rosa, Ricardo, and I had agreed that the logical thing to do was for me to sell our father's house before I returned to Miami. The house was in one of the nicest neighborhoods in Brasilia. Spacious and lovely, it had a maid's quarters, a sprawling patio and backyard, and a pool. I expected it to sell fast, but even still, when it went the first week, it caught me off-guard. The buyer wanted to move in by November, which gave me the perfect excuse for a long visit with Paulo and Dina. I found a hotel in Ipanema near Pavaozinho where we stayed for two weeks, spending most of our time at the barraca at Posto 9. Rudi and Roberta became fast friends with Paulo and Dina's children, especially Bruninho who was only a year older and, as they loved to point out, had been named after me.

CHAPTER TWENTY-THREE

Betty's Second Proposal

When we landed in Miami, Betty was waiting for us at the gate. The condo was still occupied by the renters she'd contracted, so we headed over to her house. After a long night spent in narrow airplane seats, the twins and I couldn't wait to stretch out in real beds. I remember a moment of incredible comfort, a moment of wondering whether I could actually fall asleep in full daylight, and then nothing.

When I woke, I found the twins in the kitchen with Betty. Between bites, they were explaining that peanut butter and jelly sandwiches were unheard of in Brazil. After polishing off three sandwiches between them, they ran off to look for the friends they had not seen for over a year. Thankfully no one had moved, and as only children of that age can do, they picked up right where they left off.

While they were gone, Betty said, "Bruno, I'd like to propose something to you."

I smiled, thinking back to the proposal she made me in that bar in St. Paul so long ago. "What do you have in mind? A renewal of our vows?"

"Don't make fun of me," she said, "the way you always do. This is serious. I want to adopt the twins."

My face must have given away my immediate feelings, which were that the twins were mine, not Betty's, no matter how much she liked to help. "Before you say anything," she said, "let me just say how amazed I am by the way you are with them. You know I had my doubts when you first showed up in Miami with two babies in your arms. I wasn't sure you were cut out for fatherhood. I was wrong. You're a wonderful father to them, Bruno, and I don't doubt that you could raise them on your own. They've been your babies since birth. I would never try to—I would never, ever want to undermine that or to—to replace Anthony. But watching Roberta and Rudi grow, I've felt like their mother."

"They do love you and depend on you," I said.

"It would mean a lot to me to formally be their mother. Another thing is that I have a wonderful insurance policy through my work. You should know it covers you, and if I adopt the twins, it would cover them, too."

I laughed aloud, and wrapped my arms around her shoulder. "Saint Betty," I said. "You marry me to get me a green card, and adopt my children to give them healthcare."

I kept her tucked into my side, and sat in silence. Then I said, "I never knew you felt this way, but it makes a perfect kind of sense. My only stipulation is that since they're almost eight years old now, I think they should get a say. So, you'll have to ask them."

That evening after dinner, I volunteered to do the dishes so

Betty had a window of time to talk to the twins alone. She was so tense when she called them into the living room, they immediately assumed they were in trouble.

"Did Dani say I kicked her in the shin on purpose? Because that's not true!" Roberta said.

"Don't be mad," Rudi chimed in, "she really was going for the ball. And Dani's always crying about something."

"Whatever happened with Dani, we can talk about that later. This is about something else. You both know I love you so, so much. I love you just like you're my own kids. If I adopt you, that would mean that legally, you would become my children. I'd like to do that, if you agree. What do you think?"

Silence.

"Did you tell Dad?" I could hear by the high-pitched strain in Rudi's voice that he was worried.

"Of course, honey. He was the one who told me to ask you. He wants the final decision to come from you." In response to Rudi's tension, Betty was modulating her own voice, keeping it smooth and reassuring.

"What would happen if we say yes?" asked Roberta. "Would Dad still be our Dad?"

"Of course!" Betty said. "An adoption like this would mostly just affect grownup things that have to do with laws and money. OK?" Betty asked.

"OK! OK!" they echoed.

"Come in here, Bruno!" Betty yelled. "The twins agreed! I'm the happiest person on this earth!"

One of the first things I did when we moved back into our condo was to completely remodel the roof garden. The twins were too old now for it to be a play space, and seeing it out the kitchen window reminded me too much of Anthony. Sometimes, like with that garden, the pain of his memory was just too intense to bear. Of course, even if I wanted to, it would be impossible to erase everything that reminded me of him. I had accepted that his voice would remain in my head, quieter now than when he was alive, but still chiming in every so often. Still, I wanted to look forward, not back. I took out the trees and flowers, and turned the whole thing into a vegetable garden.

Both twins continued to disappear to the soccer field whenever they got the chance. The sport was almost as popular in Miami as in Brazil. It didn't take long for everyone to notice that Roberta had a gift. Tall and graceful, with long legs, she looked almost like she was dancing when she played. Rudi was a good player, but not as good as his sister. He didn't love it in the same all-consuming way, either. My quiet son, quieter than my brother or I had ever been. I wondered sometimes what Anthony had been like as a boy, if he would have better understood Rudi, how all his inwardness would sometimes explode outward.

As Anthony had told me all too often, consequences don't count if you don't follow through. I was still prone to excuse Rudi's outbursts, an attitude that drove his teachers to distraction. After I filled Betty in on one especially aggrieved after-school meeting, she suggested that perhaps she should accompany me to future conferences. "I have another proposal for you, too," she said.

"You and your proposals," I said, smiling.

"I've thought of this for a long time," she said. "I would like to suggest that you and the twins move into this house, and live with me."

"And become a nuclear household at last."

"Ha, as if. You know I don't care about that kind of thing. What I want is for us all to fuse together, to see each other every day. I want to be around for the 'little nothing' moments, like Roberta losing her homework, or . . . I don't know yet, and that's exactly my point. You don't need to answer right away, but I want you to think about it."

"This seems logical in so many ways, but there's just—what if, well, I'm not ready to imagine meeting someone, but still, I want to feel free. Not trapped."

"Bruno, I admit I can be bossy, but please, tell me one moment during our twelve years of marriage when I have ever made you feel trapped."

"Well . . . ."

"Okay, fine, maybe you sometimes felt trapped, but I never actually stopped you from doing whatever you damn well pleased. And that won't change. All I want is to be more involved with the twins on a daily basis. You could spend more time with Rudi, I think he could use your undivided attention, and I could take Roberta to her soccer stuff. I'm learning all about the game, actually, and starting to enjoy it. And if you meet someone, you meet someone. We've dealt with that once, we could do it again."

I sighed exaggeratedly. "You're right, as always. As for housing arrangements, I need to think on it. Give me some time?"

"Take as long as you need. Maybe the twins will shoot it down, anyway."

"Don't be an idiot," I said, mussing her hair.

As it turned out, living with Betty again was easy. Having someone to share the responsibility of raising two rambunctious kids came as more of a relief than I anticipated.

∾

EPILOGUE

After a long weekend spent on the sidelines of a soccer tournament from which Roberta's select side team took home the trophy, I flipped open my laptop. Though "2009" still sounded like an impossibly futuristic time to be living in, I loved how interconnected the world had become. Despite the pleas of my children, I had become an avid Facebook user. To think that with just a click, I could see my cousin Matilda smiling on an Armacao Beach. Reality had far, far surpassed my boyhood wish for an American cousin and pen pal. I moved my cursor into the Status box. "What a life," I typed. "Beautiful weekend, beautiful kids, and even a beautiful wife, LOL. Betty found me 16 years ago and never stopped loving and accepting me just as I am. I'm a lucky guy."

About the Author

G RACEANN K. DETERS was raised in Brazil as the child of missionaries. At age 18 she returned to the U.S. where she studied nursing and received her master's in Human Development. Grace has taught nursing, counseled inmates in a men's prison, run businesses with her husband, traded securities, is fluent in Portuguese, and is an expert in Brazilian culture. Graceann is also the author of *Divine Betrayal*. She and her husband have raised three lovely daughters and now live in Incline Village, Nevada.

52856473R00152

Made in the USA
Charleston, SC
29 February 2016